9-2-70

"I
HATE
MY
PARENTS!"

Other Books by ANITA STEVENS, M.D.

ANXIETY AND DEPRESSION

by LUCY FREEMAN

FAREWELL TO FEAR
THE CRY FOR LOVE
SO YOU WANT TO BE PSYCHOANALYZED!

"I HATE MY PARENTS!"

The Real and Unreal Reasons Why Youth Is Angry

ANITA STEVENS, M.D.
and
LUCY FREEMAN

COWLES BOOK COMPANY, INC.
NEW YORK

CONTENTS

1548896

"I HATE MY PARENTS!"

1.
LOVE'S
NEW
REFRAIN

HE WALKED INTO MY OFFICE, A YOUTH TALL FOR HIS FOURTEEN years. Red wavy hair curled down to the back of his neck. His brown eyes were sensitive and intense. He sat down with an arrogant lurch on the chair across from my desk. He stared at me quizzically with his penetrating eyes.

Then he looked slowly around the room, taking in the colorful green and red abstract painting over the couch, the textbooks that occupied half a wall, the six Japanese blown-glass flower plants that lined the window sill.

"Some pad!" His voice was tinged with respect.

"Thank you." I waited for him to go on.

"So you're the shrink." An edge of contempt crept into his voice—a voice cracking with the change in tone that accompanies the slide from boyhood to manhood.

"I'm here to help you," I replied in a voice which I have been told is soft, yet firm.

"I must say you're quite a doll for a shrink." There was now admiration in the voice.

I thought I had better get on with the session, hoping he felt more at home after exchanging pleasantries. Usually anyone who faces a psychiatrist for the first time does so with some degree of apprehension at the unknown. The very word "doctor," whether of body or mind, creates fear.

"What is troubling you?" I asked.

He pursed his lips and his eyes flickered with a shade of what I construed as terror.

Then he said in a slow beat, "*They* sent me here. *They* think I'm crazy because I use pot."

"They?" I thought I knew whom he meant but wanted to be sure.

"My mother and father." There was sudden venom in his tone, the venom of a strong psychic assault.

Then the words burst from him, "I *hate* them."

"Why do you hate them?"

"Because they are always trying to put me down. They don't dig me. They think I'm some sort of puppet and all they have to do is pull the strings." His voice bespoke even greater fury within.

Then tears came to his eyes and he closed them to shut out the sight of everything except his hate.

After his session ended, a petite girl of sixteen sat in that same chair, staring at me with icy blue eyes.

"I am here because my mother and father think I'm too wild," she announced in a precise, well-modulated voice, as though she were the psychiatrist and I the confused patient.

"What do *you* think?" I asked gently.

"I do just as I please," she said defiantly. "I don't take orders from them. Their own lives are all screwed up. My father stays at his club for days if he feels like it. My mother is always screaming at him and she sleeps with the man next door, whose wife walked out on him. How dare my parents tell *me* what to do?"

"They are your parents," I pointed out.

"But I don't *have* to obey them. I don't respect them, so why should I obey them? They talk about standards, but *whose* standards? What makes them think their standards are any

2

better than mine?" Her voice was now cool as though she were talking about a theory in algebra. "They can't run their own lives but they want me to live like the Virgin Mary. I *hate* them. They're frauds."

And so it goes, the same refrain over and over: I HATE MY PARENTS. From families wealthy and poor, split and united, a lone child and a child with brothers and sisters, an underachiever and an overachiever, a withdrawn and an aggressive child, an adolescent on drugs and one who never has taken a puff of marijuana—every one who comes for help eventually says to me, without the shadow of a doubt in his voice, *"I hate my parents!"*

Not only children and adolescents but the adults I see echo the same cry, the small child still within them, as within all of us, forming a part of the inescapable past. However, children and adolescents show the intense reaction of hate much earlier because their emotions and thoughts are less buried in time.

Why is there such hatred? And why is this hatred so universal? I am certain that if I should practice in Timbuktu or Thailand or Tibet, the reaction would be the same.

Is this hate normal? Is it justified or unjustified? Is it based on real or unreal reasons? Where does it start? How can it be eased—by the child and by the parent?

Today we see widespread expression of the hatred originally sparked between child and parent in student rebellions in high schools and universities. Some demands may be reasonable but youth's violent assault on authority is not reasonable. It is the childish way of expressing temper tantrums that occurred at an earlier time of life when reason was not yet developed but which are no longer the appropriate way to ask for change.

The drug crisis, with hundreds of thousands of young

boys and girls taking marijuana, LSD, hashish, or heroin, for kicks, indicates rebellion against parents. It shows the existence of a hatred so strong that it drives the child to destruction of the self, sometimes even to death, as newspaper stories prove.

As a psychiatrist who uses psychoanalytic methods, I try to help troubled children understand that their parents are human beings, entitled to the weaknesses every human being possesses. I try to help parents understand what they are doing that is destructive to the child. Working with both child and parent, keeping them apart in the sessions, I hope to guide them toward achieving a happier life, a life in which the child no longer has to shout, "I hate my parents."

Anger is a matter of degree. The capacity for anger lies in all of us. We need it to be able to defend ourselves when we are attacked—physically or psychologically.

But there are two kinds of anger. There is the anger aroused by a realistic attack and the anger aroused by an imaginary attack. The very angry child may be rebelling against imaginary assaults, or he may, indeed, have in his home a very angry parent against whom he has to perpetually defend himself. Or the child may face both realistic *and* imaginary attacks.

Parents may become so incensed they actually will kill a child, as newspaper headlines frequently attest. Not as frequently—although it does occur—a child will kill a parent. A few years ago on the Lower East Side of Manhattan, a fifteen-year-old girl and her boyfriend stabbed her mother twenty-one times with a bread knife and encased her in limestone in the bathtub. The year before, in the Parkchester Apartments in the Bronx, a twenty-one-year-old youth fed his mother and father poisoned cocktails.

There is no such thing as a perfect parent. Freud described parenthood as one of the three "impossible professions,"

4

statesmen and psychoanalysts belonging to the other two. A parent is a human being and all human beings are imperfect. Nobody thus far has been given the kind of childhood that leads to perfection as an adult. The goal of perfection exists only in the imagination of children and emotionally immature adults.

But parents can help a child be happier if they keep in mind the fact that it is not easy to grow up. Adults often seem to forget this. A child is asked to learn in the first five years of his life to control the impulses it took man thousands of years to learn to control in order to become civilized.

A poignant picture of the hardships that face every child is described by Dr. Edward Glover, a famous psychoanalyst in Great Britain. He points out that within the first five years of life, a child has to abandon "an almost animal state of existence in favor of civilized reactions established after thousands of years of painful racial experience." States Dr. Glover:

> By the end of the first five years of life the child has weathered internal storms of love and hate; sustained profound hurts and deep disappointments; accommodated himself to an environment which is not only painfully inadequate to his hopes and fears but which, with the best or worst of intentions, may have behaved stupidly, even brutally to him. Despite these difficulties he has overcome to a large extent his boundless fears, has throttled down large charges of primitive and unteachable instinct and has directed large quantities to new goals. *Moreover—and this is perhaps the most remarkable of human achievements—he has succeeded in splitting some of his more primitive energies and has converted them into a more or less neutral form in which they can with luck be diverted towards more adapted aims.* [Italics are Dr. Glover's.]

Dr. Glover says, "with luck." But parents can shape that "luck" by understanding a child's needs. This may also mean understanding their own needs more clearly. The emotional needs of some parents are so great that they are unable to look at the child's needs as apart from their own, and may themselves need help.

Children give up primitive impulses because they want a parent's love and approval. Otherwise, they would probably remain as they are born—selfish, savage, greedy, egotistical. They learn control as what the analysts call "superego," or conscience, develops from what they are taught by parents.

One of the best ways to understand a child's needs is for a parent to try to remember the nature and quality of his own childhood and adolescence. This is difficult to do. We tend either to block out the pain and remember chiefly the pleasure, or block out the pleasure and recall chiefly the pain.

A parent should also realize that a child's mind, just like a parent's mind, and every human mind, operates on two levels—the conscious and the unconscious. While a child may be furious at his parents and aware of his rage, unconsciously he may fear his angry feelings will destroy his parents and himself if he gives in to them. Or he may fear that because he hates his parents, they will hate him instead of loving him and taking care of him, and then he will die. He needs their love to survive.

Aggression, or hate, and sexual feelings, or love, are intertwined at first. They become more separate as a child grows and he is able to distinguish between the two emotions. That is, if he is able to, which means if he is not too angry. The very angry child, the one who grows into the adult who commits murder, has never been able to love. And this means he has never known love.

While a child's anger may be caused by both conscious and unconscious factors, the unconscious ones are more difficult for both child and parent to deal with since they usually

6

revolve around feelings dangerous to one's concept of the civilized self. No one likes to think of the self as greedy, incestuous, selfish, jealous, lazy, irresponsible, murderous—which we all are in the primitive part of the self.

Anger is a danger to a child and his parents only when it is excessive. A slight occasional rebellion by a child may be part of his growing up, his attempt to be free of parents to whom he feels very close. Parents should allow the child to be himself, not insist he be a carbon copy of them. They should not demand that he control his every spark of rage. They should permit him expression of his natural anger when they frustrate him which, to civilize him, they must do at times.

It invariably occurs, with the children I see, that as they admit and accept their hate for parents, they become aware— perhaps for the first time—of their great love and need for their parents, and their need to be understood and accepted by their parents. The feeling of mixed love and hate for one person is called "ambivalence." I try to help children and youth understand the ambivalence in their hearts as we also try to find out whether their hatred is based on real or unreal causes.

Dr. Karl Abraham, one of the pioneer psychoanalysts, said that the goal of psychic help was to enable a patient to master ambivalence. This means that the child or young person must accept his feelings of both love and hate for a mother and father, and his *right* to those feelings. A growing ability to handle whatever feelings of hate he may have will follow.

Excessive hate is a sign of weakness; the weak cannot accept authority of any kind, not even when it is wise and sympathetic. The therapist's goal is to strengthen the young person's image of himself so he feels strong enough to accept an authority he really needs.

7

When a young person feels emotionally weak, he will hate those closest to him—his parents. They are his first love and his first hate. He is apt to misbehave at home rather than in school or with playmates. He will hate his parents more than a stranger; he may turn to a stranger hoping the stranger will understand him better than his parents do. For, with a stranger there is hope—a hope he feels has been destroyed at home. That is one reason therapy works, if the youngster is fortunate enough to find a stranger skilled in understanding his emotional needs.

I hope harmony and peace are already on their way when a child enters my waiting room. Because I see so many children (about half my practice consists of adolescents and younger boys and girls), I have tried to decorate my waiting room and office in a serene, restful way that is pleasurable to the eye.

The waiting room is small but inviting, with the emphasis on warmth and intimacy. I chose quiet colors—subtle variations of blue and green. The doors are turquoise with three wood-carved plaques lacquered in the same color, contrasting with the white walls. The furniture is modern and comfortable. (Too many psychiatrists furnish their offices from leftovers at home, using various oddments their wives do not want around the house or apartment.)

On the wall hangs a colorful abstract painting by a young artist, Michon, which I bought at an exhibit in Montreal. The abstract in my office is also by Michon. The one in the waiting room looks like a silhouette of New York or any large city; adjacent to it hang several Japanese prints. The abstract in my office, according to one patient, could be a colorful representation of the unconscious. One can see what one wants in abstract paintings. They are a prod to hidden feelings.

Children most often notice the replicas of animals standing around the room—a bronze donkey, a golden goat, a glass pig, the three famous monkeys—*See no Evil, Hear no Evil, Speak no Evil*—a brass dog, and a copper owl. A small candy-striped dog is the gift of Roark Bradford, author of *Ol' Man Adam an' His Chillun* and a friend of mine. A small cactus growing in a glass bowl is the gift of a tiny patient; often children will bring presents as a thank-you.

One nine-year-old girl said admiringly, "This can't be a doctor's office! It's more like a home." And that is just the impression I try to convey with the décor of my office. I want my patients, young and old, to feel they are in friendly surroundings. I hope that by feeling comfortable they will be able to focus on the task at hand—understanding themselves.

As the young person's awareness of his own identity grows, he realizes that, if his parents have done nothing else, they have at least fed, sheltered, and clothed him from the day he was born. He also discovers that, while he may have suffered somewhat because of their emotional deficiencies, he has to learn to be responsible for his own acts.

At the very point the young person begins to appreciate who he is and accepts that he is *entitled* to harbor both love and hate for his mother and father, he becomes willing to acknowledge the love. Before this he has been able to scream out only his hate.

The cry *"I hate my parents!"* then changes to "I also love and need my parents," as the young person understands his parents want the very best for him. The fact they have brought him to my office so he may feel happier is proof of their love.

2.
OUR
TURNED-ON
YOUTH

I SMOKE CIGARETTES. THE YOUNG PEOPLE WHO STREAM INTO my office smoke pot.

I asked one sixteen-year-old boy, "Why do you smoke pot?"

He replied, "I get too uptight without grass, Doc." Then he asked bluntly, "Why don't you smoke grass instead of cigarettes?" He indicated the ashtray on my desk, used sometimes between patients, or when talking on the telephone, but never when a patient is in the room.

I laughed. "I'm too old for grass."

We can no longer ignore youth's scream for help which, in a sense, is the cry of the drug addict.

The drug scene is part of today's culture. Hundreds of young people on drugs come to my office, sent by physicians or parents for treatment or consultation. The drugs they take range all the way from the supposedly innocuous marijuana, or pot, to the more dangerous acid (LSD), the amphetamines, cocaine, and heroin.

Estimates vary as to what extent youth is involved in drug-taking. Some place high school and college drug users as high as 50 per cent. This includes youngsters who either are on drugs daily or have experimented once.

The young addicts come from all walks of life. A twelve-year-old Harlem youth recently died of an overdose of heroin. A governor's son was arrested on the charge of possessing marijuana. Eleven-year-old boys in Brooklyn were charged with being pushers. In New York City in the first eleven months of 1969, a total of 7,352 youths between sixteen and twenty were arrested on misdemeanor charges involving drugs.

I have been asked if the legalization of marijuana would help. Those who advocate it point to the desperate days when liquor was illegal and sold by bootleggers. Will the legalization of drugs take the pressure off troubled youth?

I do not think there is anything in this world that can protect a human being from all contingencies. If someone wants to swallow a potion or take a pill which he believes will lessen his unhappiness, he will find that potion or pill. Today drugs are available as a psychic painkiller. Why is there no restriction, for instance, on aspirin? A number of boys and girls have tried to commit suicide with aspirin because the bottle is so handy, in practically every medicine chest.

There are those who claim pot is more harmful than alcohol. Alcohol has medicinal value, and it is breaking no law to drink whisky. We do not know whether pot has medicinal value or whether it is destructive to parts of the body, for not enough long-term research has been done. We also do not know whether the taking of pot invariably leads to more dangerous drugs like speed and acid. Some say it does, others, that it does not. Whether pot is addictive is controversial. No one knows for sure.

There is virtually no completely validated information on the biological hazards of drugs such as LSD, marijuana, amphetamines, barbiturates, and opiates, despite their widespread use.

Leading scientists reported this at a conference on the

11

nonpsychiatric hazards of drug abuse held recently in San Francisco.

Most studies concerning these drugs have focused on their psychopharmacological effects. But their potential for biological damage—primarily cancer, fetal destruction, and genetic changes—is great. This was the conclusion of twenty scientists at a two-day conference sponsored by the Center for Studies of Narcotic and Drug Abuse of the Department of Health, Education and Welfare's National Institute of Mental Health and the Environmental Mutagen Society.

The twenty scientists agreed that drugs of abuse pose special problems for study including:

(1) Increasing numbers of adults of child-bearing age are using drugs over a prolonged period.

(2) The drugs are frequently injected rather than ingested.

(3) More than one drug is often used.

(4) Drug preparations are often crude, resulting in discrepancies in test data on pure and "back-street" drugs.

(5) Validating dosage is difficult.

(6) These drugs are highly active biologically at subtoxic concentrations.

(7) Infection and malnutrition are usually prevalent in user populations.

(8) Legal obstacles limit the availability of these drugs for scientific study.

LSD has received more study as to its potential for biological damage than other drugs of abuse. But much of the data on the effects of LSD is conflicting, making it impossible to draw any firm conclusions as to its safety, said the scientists.

It is known that heroin is harmful and more younger people are using it. In New York City in 1950 the mean age of those who died from using heroin was thirty-five years. In

12

1969, it had dropped to a little over twenty-three years. Of the more than 900 heroin users who died in the city in 1969, 224 were teen-agers and one was only twelve.

After heroin addiction, the user cannot turn off as easily as he once turned on. According to Dr. Harvey Gollance, Associate Director of the Beth Israel Medical Center in New York and head of the methadone program there, studies demonstrate that heroin addiction causes a change in the body cells. The result is that once a person is addicted, he may experience "drug hunger" for years to come, possibly the rest of his life, if he lives very long. The tragic effects of heroin on a youth who became an addict, seduced by a young woman into taking the drug, were graphically portrayed in the movie *More*. Doctors explain that one of the dangers is that when it enters the bloodstream, heroin causes a precipitous decline in respiration.

Teen-agers who once felt daring if they smoked, or sneaked a cocktail in the kitchen, now obtain that same sense of daring by smoking pot or taking a "trip" with LSD. But cigarettes and alcohol are quite a different story from drugs, which are illegal. Thus the taking of drugs constitutes defiance of the law, which to the rebellious youngster adds a thrill.

The important question to ask is why so many young people, even nine-year-olds, are "turning on"?

As I examine and listen to the many boys and girls who visit my office for help, there seems to be only one conclusion. They are all emotionally disturbed young people with a deep need to relieve underlying anxiety and depression. In their own phrase, taking narcotics is a "cop-out."

In varying words, the customary excuse given to me is, "I take drugs because when I'm high I forget that I'm depressed."

Psychoanalyst Dr. Bruno Bettelheim has aptly called drugs

13

"the instant mother" for young people, "the nurturing mother they never had."

A former addict, now seventeen, echoes this assessment, saying, "Drugs are a return to the womb, you feel warm, enclosed, safe. You have to be super-sick to take them. I stopped because I felt I had wallowed long enough in childish self-pity."

Arnold A. Rogow, in his book *The Psychiatrists*, has this to say about hippies and their drug hangups:

> The hippie, to most psychiatrists, is a disturbed individual who experiences himself, as one psychiatrist has written with reference to alienated college students, "as being detached from his own feelings as well as from those around him." In addition to using drugs such as marihuana and LSD, and being sexually promiscuous, the hippie tends to live in the present, avoiding commitment to people, causes, and ideas. He is unable or unwilling to communicate with his parents or other adults. Because his self-concept is ill-defined and confused, anxiety is "pervasive and relentless," leading toward severe depressions that may be accompanied by suicide attempts. When seen by a psychiatrist, he is apt to complain of "apathy, boredom, meaninglessness, and chronic unhappiness." Although he may be far above average in intelligence, he is unable to concentrate on his studies or achieve more than low grades.

In the main, depression and anxiety stem from the relationship to parents. But they may be made more intense by the pressures of the world in which we live, the go-go world, the world in which nations are taking part in undeclared wars all over the globe. The children of our time have far more material advantages than children of previous generations, but because of the age of anxiety in which we live they seem to get less understanding and attention from parents, or the wrong kind of attention.

14

Often nobody is at home to listen. Or, when parents are at home, they are too busy with their own lives to *really listen*. I have seen such parents in my office—the mother who will not stop crying, the father who will not stop talking, as they complain about their drug-ridden child. As I try to get a word in, I realize what the child is up against at home. The mother's tears make him feel guilty, the father does not talk to him but *at* him in a preachy way.

My heart goes out to these youngsters as they stream into my office, one after the other, and lay bare their innermost thoughts. Often they are relieved *just to be able to talk to somebody, anybody, about what they feel.*

One of the most important things a parent can give a child is *time*. Many young people are suffering because a mother or father will not take the time to listen, but brushes them off with, "Later." Or, "There's no time now." It's wait, wait, wait, and youth is not a time of waiting. This is for adulthood.

After all, what is it that a psychiatrist does that helps a child or adult? He *listens*. He does more, for he possesses those special skills needed to give emotional help. But first, to win the trust of the patient, and in order to get a picture of his background, the psychiatrist *listens*.

Over and over I hear each youngster say in awe, after the first session, "This is the first time in my whole life anyone has ever listened to me."

One mother who intuitively sensed the importance of listening saw her five-year-old son outside the house bargaining with another little boy. He finally accepted from the other boy a small, dirty turtle. He bore the turtle into the house with an ecstatic smile on his face.

He rushed over to his mother as though holding a precious pearl in his palm, and said in awe, "Look at him!"

15

"He's very nice," she said, inwardly grimacing. "Where did you get him?"

"Harvey gave him to me in a bargain. He said I could have his turtle if I would make him a member of my baseball team."

The mother thought a minute, then said, knowing Harvey's family did not have much money, "Suppose we buy Harvey another turtle and you *still* make him a member of your team."

The son thought a moment, then replied, "Okay. I think Harvey would like that."

That night when her husband came home from his law office, she drew him aside, warned, "Please listen when Toby tells you about the bargain he made today."

Her husband's mouth opened in protest. "I have more important things to think about than what that kid—"

"No, you don't," she insisted quietly. "His little turtle means just as much to him as your million-dollar lawsuit does to you."

Her husband looked surprised, then nodded his head in understanding. "I guess you're right," he said. "I never thought of it that way."

Listening alone is not enough. It is also important that during times of crisis the parent listen without reacting emotionally to what is being said. Because of the complicated relationship between parent and child, a parent is apt to explode in anger when he is upset by something his child has done, instead of trying to understand the child's reasons for his act.

"Dad, I took a puff of grass today to see what it felt like," a fourteen-year-old dared confide in his father, hoping the father would share his experience with him, talk to him about the pros and cons of drugs.

"Why, you little bastard!" the father screamed. "After

16

all I've done for you. I should wallop you good. If you ever dare touch that stuff again, I'll have your hide."

The boy was aghast. He had not dreamed his father would react so violently. His self-esteem was shattered because of the verbal beating and instead of giving up smoking, as well he might have if his father had reasoned with him, he could not wait until his next joint, and his next.

It was not necessary for this father to condone his son's taking drugs but he should have heard him out, accepted the boy's feelings about smoking, and then tried to reason with him.

Youth is bound to have a different point of view on many things, including morality, marriage, education, and money. Often young people only test out ideas on parents. They want to hear the older generation's beliefs presented in a thoughtful way, in a courteous voice, rather than in an angry, dictatorial manner.

Many young people might have avoided becoming addicted to drugs if they had parents who cared enough to listen to them.

A fourteen-year-old boy, accustomed to seeing his father come home at night with a stack of economic books behind which he would barricade himself in the study, passed his father in the hall one evening and said sadly, "Hi, Dad. Remember me?"

A fifteen-year-old girl was brought to my office by her uncle and aunt at whose home she lived, because of delinquent behavior. She often stayed out all night, sleeping with strange young men she picked up on the street; she smoked pot, and stole money from her aunt. She was living with her aunt and uncle by order of the court because her mother was in a mental institution and her father was an alcoholic and out of work most of the time.

17

When I saw the girl, she said, "Who cares *what* I do? Nobody ever listens to me. My aunt and uncle are always too busy, and really, why should they care? They have their own lives to lead. And besides, they belong to another generation."

There *is* a generation gap. And allow it to be, I tell parents. Go down to the level of your children. Do not insist they come up to yours. For they are unable to do so.

No child is born "bad." It is what happens to him from the day he is born that determines whether he will later get into trouble. We do not know, as yet, enough about the very early life of children. Too much is forgotten, repressed by the child and by the parents. When children think they remember, it often turns out to be a screen memory (a recall that hides the more deeply buried memory of an earlier, more traumatic experience).

Anxiety begins the day we are born and is enhanced by what happens between parent and child. Children may be born with different dispositions, one child showing the aggression of a tiger, another acting as placidly as a cow. But chiefly, it is what happens to a child and his mother's and father's reactions to him that determine his emotional growth.

Because our "man on the moon" culture has progressed to such a high level of speed, children who start off insecure are apt to feel even more insecure. A child today is born into a world far more sophisticated and speedy than the child of ten years ago. Too much understanding may be demanded of children too early, with not enough patience present to allow them to grow slowly into this rocket age.

I feel sorry for both child and parent when a child is troubled. What could be closer to the hearts of parents than their own flesh and blood, the little people they are raising? To say there is no communication between a parent and a child is tragic. For parents should be the child's best friends, and the child should be the parents' best friend.

This does not mean parents should burden a child with their problems. Once in a while a boy or girl will walk into my office with the face of a little old man or woman. I know this child has been asked to accept psychic burdens far beyond his capacity. He has grown up too quickly.

Nor should parents complain to the child of their anxiety. When a parent says, "I feel depressed," or "I am sick," the child, because of his natural feelings of omnipotence (all children feel the world revolves around them alone), will think he is responsible for the depression or the illness and feel guilty, punishing himself in fantasy.

I remember what a devastating blow it was to me when my father died. I went straight from the funeral to my office, where I had to see troubled patients. But I never showed one sign of grief to a patient, for that would have placed an unnecessary burden on him. Nor should a parent show grief to a child.

In general, a parent should ask, "How can I strengthen, not shatter, my child's ego? How can I help him grow up more easily?" And one way is to let the child show you how—by listening to him.

Many a youth tells me he will go to a parent and ask a question—any question, maybe about sex or money, maybe about how to cope with a tyrannical teacher—and the parent will put him off, saying, "It's your bedtime. We'll talk about it tomorrow," or "I'm busy now. Later." Or, about sex, "You wouldn't understand. Ask me again when you're older."

Such answers infuriate a youngster. They cause enormous frustration, for his psychic growth depends, in part, on getting answers, or at least *knowing his question has been heard*. To postpone discussion is to scoff at him.

There comes to mind a very extreme case, but it shows clearly how one son was ignored and mistreated and illustrates why many of our young people are taking to drugs.

19

A sixteen-year-old boy named Rick, the son of a Wall Street broker, was referred to me by a physician because the youth had run away from home. He had lived in the East Village in a hippie pad where he took pot daily. (As one psychiatrist has commented, the very word "pot" is appropriate since it is a word symbolizing the toilet-training stage, showing the infantile nature of addicts.)

This tall, handsome youth entered my office like a prisoner between two guards. His mother marched on one side, his father on the other. They were dressed expensively, as was he. After the introductory pleasantries, I asked them to wait outside while I talked to him.

Rick wore a conservative navy blue suit, a conventional blue and white striped necktie, and a white starched shirt. He looked uncomfortable and kept rubbing his neck, red and itchy from the starch of the collar. His hair, of moderate length, was brushed back from his wide forehead. He sat stiffly in the chair, seeming to resent being there; he was as tense as he looked in his obviously new clothes.

His first words were an apology-attack. "They made me cut my hair just to see you."

Knowing the scornful "they" referred to his parents, I asked, "Is that what you usually wear?" gesturing at his attire.

He grinned. "I'm afraid to tell you what I usually wear."

"What about wearing your usual clothes when you come to see me the next time," I said, adding, "that is, if you wish to come again."

"I'll dress that way if you fix it with my parents so they won't object," he said. Then he added hastily, too hastily, "They're really wonderful people. They're not like parents. They're more like friends."

Later, when I interviewed his mother and father as he waited outside, they told me they first suspected Rick was

20

smoking pot because he was associating in school "with long-haired, wild-looking boys known to be drug addicts."

"Rick has always been honest with us, so we asked if he smoked pot," said the father, tall like his son, and well built, although he had a nervous manner. The mother, also nervous, spoke in a high, screechy voice.

"What did he say?" I asked.

"He admitted he had taken pot," replied the father.

"What did you do?" I asked.

"I hit him," said the father righteously. "I took off my belt and I gave it to him good."

The mother put in, "Then we made him come home right after school for two weeks as a punishment and forbade him ever to speak to those boys again."

"What happened after that?" I asked.

"He wouldn't study. His teachers said he just sat in class, staring into space. He started to look pale and lost his spark. Then he flunked his finals, and had to repeat the year," said the father.

"And that's when we asked our doctor what to do and he sent us to you," added the mother.

"Do you want me to see him again?" I queried.

"Please," they chorused.

"Next time I would like him to dress as he usually dresses," I said. "I want to see what he customarily wears."

The father hesitated, then said, "All right. If that's what you wish."

At Rick's next session, as he walked in, I hardly recognized him. He wore dirty blue jeans, a white T-shirt, sandals without socks, and his hair was long and uncombed. "It's me, Doc," he said with a winning grin. "Do you mind the garb?"

"I asked you to dress the way you usually do," I reminded him. "Please sit down."

"It sure was a pleasure to leave that hell-hole today," he said.

"Hell-hole?" I was puzzled.

"My home. Where I live."

"Where is that?"

"It's a whole town house on East Sixty-fifth Street. My parents think it's quite a pad. But I call it the hell-hole."

He was sitting stiffly in the chair. I asked, "Is that the way you usually sit?"

"No. This is how I usually sit." He sprawled out his long legs and slouched down in the chair, looking at me as if not sure what I would do to him for assuming such a careless, defiant posture.

"Please make yourself comfortable," I said.

"I sure feel more like me this way," he remarked.

"Tell me about yourself," I suggested.

"My mother and father don't understand me at all. Truthfully, I wouldn't care if I never saw them again. Mother nags all the time. If I stay up half an hour late at night, she's in my room, pecking away with stupid questions like, 'Why aren't you in bed?' or 'What are you doing?' She's always complaining to me about something I do wrong. My father? When he feels like it, he'll take off his belt and hit me. I hate him. He can't know how much I hate him!"

This was a far cry from the first session when Rick told me, "My parents are wonderful people. They're not like parents. They're more like friends."

He went on, "Whenever I ask a question, they brush me off. They punish me by making me stay in my room after school when I don't obey them. They treat me like dirt, Doc. When I hear Dad talking about a big deal at the office and ask him about it, Mother says, 'Stay out of this, Rick. It's not your business.' "

22

He told me how one day he gave in to the urging of his friends at school and tried pot. Then, when his parents asked him about it, he told the truth.

"And what did I get? A beating from Dad. And now I've lost my friends because my parents forbid me to speak to them. I have nobody. I feel lost, Doc."

I could not help thinking of what Freud said, that, to preserve a healthy, sane mind, one has to avoid loneliness and to feel a certain self-respect (what Freud called a strong ego). Rick's ego had been crushed by insensitive parents who constantly criticized him, made him feel nothing he did was right. There was no one in whom he could confide. Therefore he sank into a depression, not daring to display his anger at his mother and father. Intense depression, as we know, is a way of denying unrecognized murderous feelings. It is the wish to murder turned inward on the self.

Rick was talking on in a rush, as though he had to get out all his feelings at once. "Then one day, I found I couldn't study any more. I didn't want to learn. It was too much effort. I flunked the finals and was put back a year. One of my old friends, the ones I was forbidden to see, came over and said, 'Rick, what's happened to you? You're not the same as you used to be. You're too down, man. Come on and have a few joints with us.' And I thought, 'What have I got to lose?' So I went to this boy's house and we smoked pot and I felt fine once again. But I was nervous as hell, worrying what would happen if my parents found out. I was sure they were having me trailed, that they knew everything I did."

He had sneaked away a few months before, he said, to another friend's house but did not have a peaceful moment as the rest of them smoked pot. He refused, sat in a corner of the room. The others called him "chick." They said, "You don't belong here, man. You're an odd-ball." He started to cry. One of the boys walked over to him, handed him a joint, said, "We want you to be one of us," and he smoked pot and felt a sense of relief for the moment.

He began to smoke pot more and more. Pot helped him overcome depression. Pot was associated with his "friends," not his punishing parents.

Then came the showdown. "One night I stayed out all night with my friends. I slept at the house of one, whose mother and father said they would rather have their son smoke pot at home than on the street. When I went home the next evening, my father"—Rick choked at the memory, then went on—"my father knocked me down the stairs. He said, 'We're finished with you. You're disowned. Leave this house and never come near us again.' "

He was silent a moment, then continued, "I didn't know where to go. I went to a mental health clinic for help. They said I had to get my parents' permission before they would give me any assistance. I didn't want to get in touch with my parents about anything. So I went to live with a friend for a while but I knew it wouldn't be fair to his parents to stay long. I drifted down to the Village; it was summer and I found a congenial group of hippies and lived with them in a pad. But not for long. My parents evidently had second thoughts. They sent the police after me and brought me home."

He sighed. "School started and I had to study each night. My father would make me sit with him in the library. He would drink his cocktail and read his paper and stare at me over the edge of it to make sure I was studying. I sweated pure agony. Whenever I heard his footsteps approaching the library, I shuddered. I hated the old man."

A son has a natural enmity for a father because of his Oedipal feelings, but Rick's enmity was intense because his father beat him, threw him down a flight of stairs, shouted, "Get out!"

"And my mother—I can't stand that voice, it cuts through me. I think I'll go crazy with those two."

And with these words, the tall youth broke into sobs that wracked his slim body. I handed him a facial tissue, waited until the sobs subsided, and gave him a look of sympathy.

"I'm sorry, Doc," he said. "But you don't know what it's like to have parents standing over you like sentinels."

I said quietly, "Do you mind if I speak to your parents about the way they are treating you?"

"I've reached the point, Doc, where if you tell my parents everything I said, it can't be any worse for me. If I can't get pot, I don't want to live. I don't think I could bear it."

He was telling me his depression was so deep, he found it unbearable. I said, "If you let me talk to your parents without revealing anything that will incriminate you, I promise you things will get better, or I will have failed you."

Then I asked, curious, "Where do you get the money for pot?"

"My allowance is cut off but my friends give me joints free. They always have plenty."

"I won't say a word to your parents about your smoking pot," I reassured him. Nor did I lecture him about taking pot. I wanted only to listen to what he had to say, wanted him to be able to ventilate his feelings after all the years of silence and abuse and stored-up rebellion.

"Can I come back tomorrow?" he asked. "I have a lot more to tell you."

I was pleased that he wanted to return so promptly. I fit him into a busy schedule, thinking it important not to refuse his request.

During the next several sessions, he asked over and over, "Will I be punished the rest of my life because I'm doing something against my parents' wishes? Pot makes me feel good. Why can't I use it?"

25

I tried to help him realize his parents at heart were not his enemies, that they were trying their best to keep him from harm, that they honestly believed they loved him.

"I love them, too," he said, his voice desperate with longing. "That's part of my hangup. I love them and I hate them."

After several weeks, when I called his parents, I found them eager to talk to me. The father said, half in admiration, half in resentment, "I see quite a change in my son. He whistles when he comes home. He goes to bed on time. We have no fights now."

Rick *had* improved, according to his parents' values, I thought. But I also wondered if they were not fearful of what he might be revealing to me about them. Because of the drastic change in their son's behavior, perhaps they were becoming aware that at times they acted irrationally.

They asked if they could see me for suggestions as to what they might do to help. After they were seated in my office, before I could say a word, the father blurted out, "Dr. Stevens, there's a great change in my son. What did I do wrong?"

I asked, "Did you ever strike your son in anger?"

"Yes," he admitted and blushed.

His wife screeched at him, "I always told you not to use the belt on that kid."

He turned on her in wrath. "And you tell Dr. Stevens how often I told you to stop screaming at him over nothing."

I talked to them quietly, tried to aid them in understanding their son's need to be himself, reach his own decisions, make his own errors, just as, when I talked to him, I tried to help him understand his parents as human beings with frailties.

After six months of talking about his innermost feelings, Rick had forgotten he ever took pot. He told me, "I'm sorry for kids who have to live in a dream world. They're trying to kick reality, and it can't be done."

His parents had stopped nagging him about what he wore, what he did, whom he saw. They allowed him to come and go as he wished. They both went into therapy, which helped ease the situation considerably. As Rick lost much of his anger at them, a new feeling of ease settled over the household.

At the end of a year's treatment, Rick's marks in school were excellent, he had a girl with whom he went steady, and he was enjoying life. He still wore his hair long but kept it neat.

Here it was clear that a youth took drugs to try to overcome an underlying depression. In most cases parents are not as punitive as Rick's. Fathers do not hit sons with a belt nor mothers nag at them constantly. Yet boys and girls still resort to drugs. Which means they are depressed for other reasons.

Some parents cannot say "no" to a child. This, too, is harmful. Love is not to be confused with permissiveness. Love holds in it acceptance but, in the case of parent and child, it also means guidance and protection. It is always the way something is said to a child, rather than what is said. One parent may say thoughtfully, "I would rather you didn't do that," whereas another may scream, "I forbid you to do that!" It is human nature to return thoughtfulness with thoughtfulness, anger with anger.

Most important are the standards set by parents. Alcoholic parents have no right to demand that their child refrain from taking drugs. Children caricature parents to a great extent, going them one better most of the time.

We have in this nation an epidemic not of drug addicts but of unhappy young people. Some are easily induced to take drugs by a friend who has found relief. Some feel it is the thing to do and "you just chicken out if you don't try it," as one thirteen-year-old girl said. Then there are those who might wish to try pot but are afraid of what their parents would think.

The boy or girl who tries smoking pot and then gives it up, or only smokes occasionally when he does not want to feel alienated from the crowd, is usually the one able to talk frankly with his parents about drugs and the one not fighting depression or anxiety. He has parents who will, in all probability, quietly point out that it is illegal to smoke marijuana and that pot solves no problems but may be destructive physically and mentally. After all, why should any drug be needed to sustain a young life? Just being alive should be challenge enough.

"Reality is the real trip," as Shane Stevens, author of *Go Down Dead,* the searing story of a youth in Harlem, says.

Parents should be careful that they do not accuse a child of being an addict when he has only experimented with pot. A fifteen-year-old girl who had been suspended from school and whose parents were highly condemnatory was accused of being an addict. She had fallen ill with hepatitis and the pot was blamed.

"But I've only smoked twice," she said to me. "I don't think that caused the hepatitis."

I wondered if she had caught hepatitis any other way. I asked questions about where she had eaten.

"I love fish, especially clams," she confessed. "I often go down to a place in the Village and eat clams by the dozens."

"Next time you're there, find out if anyone who has eaten there regularly has contracted hepatitis from the clams," I suggested. Raw fish has been known to cause it.

She walked in jubilant for her next session. "Six people who eat in that restaurant regularly have hepatitis!" she announced.

"Tell your parents not to jump to conclusions about you

as a drug addict," I said. "Two times does not an addict make."

The drug addict operates solely on the pleasure principle. He wants gratification of sensual pleasure *now*, without endeavor, without effort. Life does not work that way. We have to earn our pleasure. Part of pleasure lies in the way we gain it and the anticipation of it.

The young person who depends on drugs to get through the day is apt to be withdrawn and introverted, finding it difficult to express his anger (always a symptom of depression). The drug removes some of the censors of the mind and gives him the ability to be paranoid—the world, society, his parents, are all against him, he feels. A little paranoia is not a dangerous thing. We all possess the ability to feel paranoid in order to save our life when we feel something threatens it. Paranoia is part of our psychic life-saving machinery. It is only when we excessively fear fantasied threats that paranoia becomes a problem.

With young persons who are addicted to drugs, the first goal is to reduce the anxiety and depression which is driving them to drugs.

All youngsters who take drugs day after day—whether pot, speed, or acid—possess emotional conflicts and need help. The drug scene in a sense quickly pinpoints for us our troubled children. They say they take the drugs to get "kicks." But they would not need "kicks" if they were not emotionally disturbed. They may be doing their own thing. But their thing is destructive.

Drug users claim they find an "identity" through turning on. But you can find your identity only without drugs. Drugs distort identity.

Today the "square" stands out as the brave one.

3.
THE
"GOOD"
CHILD

THE DRUG ADDICTS ARE OPEN REBELS. BUT MANY YOUNGSTERS wear a mask of meekness and compliance, outwardly obeying every command of a parent, spoken or unspoken, not daring to rebel. They live a life of inner terror.

Such youths need to be helped to express their anger. They have to become strong enough psychically to want to be independent, to wish to break free of the domination of parents. Heretofore restrained "good" little boys and girls, they have to be encouraged to know what it feels like in their bones to risk a parent's disapproval and wrath. They need to sow a few psychic oats.

Excessive "goodness" over the years may cause a youth to hate his parents unreasonably. For, when feelings of rage are suppressed too intensely, they may erupt in a dangerous way for both child and parent. Far better that anger simmers out as it is felt, when both child and parent are able to deal with it more easily.

A youth of thirteen was sent to me by a physician who had failed to persuade the boy to break a hunger strike. This physician advised the parents to consult a psychiatrist and gave them my name.

Terry had long blond hair, like a girl's, which curled in

ringlets around his cherubic face. His blue eyes held an innocence carried from the cradle, as he looked at me.

"What do I talk about?" he asked.

"Anything you wish." I settled back in my chair to listen, to try to find the psychic clues that would expose the reasons why he refused to eat.

Terry's mother had informed me on the telephone, her voice a low wail, "We can't understand Terry's behavior. He's always been a good boy. We have raised him to be a devout Catholic. He goes to church and confession regularly. We love him dearly. He is our only child."

What had happened over the thirteen years of Terry's life that he should suddenly refuse to eat a morsel of food, preferring to die rather than live? What sudden terror did he face, terror about which he could speak to no one?

But he was speaking now. "My mother and father sent me to you because they thought you could make me eat." In his voice I caught a slight note of hope, as if he wished this, too.

"I wouldn't *make* you do anything," I said.

"Really?" Those big eyes opened wider.

"I don't believe in *making* people do things. But I try to understand why they are doing things that are harmful to them. Like your hunger strike."

Silence.

Then he said, "They're trying to poison me."

"Oh?" I tried to hide my surprise. As a rule, it is difficult for me to register shock after years of facing troubled men, women, and children beset by all sorts of bizarre, twisted fantasies of the mind.

"I won't eat because the food is poisoned." His voice held an emphatic tone, the sureness of those trapped in delusion, needing the delusion because the psychic reality is too painful.

31

Why did he believe his parents wanted to poison him, that he was not worth keeping alive? What crime did he think he had committed that he deserved death? Also, since his wish to commit suicide by starvation was an outgrowth of his original wish to murder, why did he want to kill his mother and father?

I did not ask this directly, of course, for a child is usually not aware of such a wish, or if he is, it is a fleeting thought, and to bring it up would alarm him or fortify his defenses so he would become even more emotionally upset.

"Is anything bothering you at the moment?" I asked.

He bit his lips, looked away.

"You can tell me anything," I said. "I'm a doctor. I want to help you."

He looked back at me, trust showing in his eyes. "It was the priest," he said, then again looked away, out the window at the budding trees in Central Park.

"What did the priest do?" I thought, perhaps, the priest might have told Terry's parents something the boy had divulged during confession.

"It was what he said to me."

"What did he say?"

"I told him that I had touched myself, you know . . . down there . . . and . . ." the young voice trembled, stopped.

"What did he say?" I repeated gently.

"He said, 'You will go insane.'"

I sighed. I thought such witches' tales had long been abolished, exposed to the light of reason. But no, children were still being fed such frightening psychic stuff, and I thought of Terry's refusal to "eat."

"But it's not true," I assured him.

"It isn't?" He sounded as if he wanted to believe me but dared not.

32

"Of course it isn't true. If it were true, there would not be a sane person in the world. It is perfectly natural for every boy and girl to want to explore their body at a certain time of life. If they didn't, there would be something wrong with them."

"Gosh!" His relief was evident.

"Priests aren't always right. They have their problems, too. Remember, they are human like you and me."

He stared intently at me, this youngster who had never before dared disobey his mother or father, whose behavior had been too good to be true. Slowly the tension in his face dissolved and he flashed me a look of gratitude, as though I had unwrapped chains encircling his body. Children can be very direct in expression of emotion, if they are allowed to be free and natural.

Taking a cue from Terry's revelation, I asked, "Was what the priest said connected to your refusal to eat?"

The words gushed out. "If I was that bad, if touching myself meant I would go insane, then my mother and father would want to kill me."

"Why would they want to kill you for being insane?" I was puzzled.

"Well, when Uncle Ted went insane and then died last month, my mother said to my father, 'It's better Ted should die than that he live and be crazy.' "

There is always a kind of logic behind the fantasy—what Freud called "a fragment of truth." Many a belief of a child, no matter how mad it sounds, is founded on some fact of his life, perhaps something his mother or father said or did or even just felt, communicating the feeling by a sneer or a tear or a silence.

After Terry left my office, I called his mother and told her what he had said. She burst into tears.

"There *is* insanity in the family," she said. "My brother Ted suddenly lost his mind and died of a cerebral hemorrhage. But I didn't dream Terry would think what I said about Ted applied to him!"

"You couldn't know what the priest would say," I reassured her. "Let's see if Terry eats his supper tonight."

She called the next day to report Terry had devoured every bit of food set before him and asked for a second helping of chocolate cake. Her voice was exultant. "You are marvelous! It's a miracle! Not even the regular doctor could do that."

I smiled to myself. Many people do not understand what is involved in treatment of the mind, which is different from treatment of the body. It is not something done *to* anyone. It is something done *with* them.

I said, "It's no miracle at all. Terry just was able to speak about what was tormenting him."

"Why doesn't he tell *me*?" Her voice was petulant.

"It is sometimes difficult for children to talk to a parent about the things that alarm them," I replied. "They are afraid they will lose the parent's love if they reveal themselves as less than perfect."

"I am worried to death about Terry," she confessed. "Did you notice how long his hair is? Can't you get him to cut it?"

"Then he wouldn't be like the other boys."

She seemed not to hear. "And those horrible blue jeans. He won't wear decent trousers."

"Most boys his age wear blue jeans."

"And he has such dreadful friends. Like that sloppy Charley Smith. Can't you talk him out of playing with Charley?"

"Don't you think Terry has a right to his own friends?"

"And he's always late to school and . . ."

The complaints about Terry went on and on. I began to

understand what this boy's life had been like at home—an
only child, target of his mother and father's "thou shalt nots,"
with no chance to make his own choices. All of this meant he
would be hiding a murderous rage at his parents behind the
mask of goodness and obedience. He would have liked to
poison *them*. His fear of being poisoned was in part projection
of his own wish.

He came to see me twice a week and slowly the mask
started to fall. He talked about things that had been troubling
him over the uncertain years.   1548896

"Is it right that my mother throws it in my face all the
time that she has given up her career as a singer for me, that
she cooks for me, takes care of me, like I'm her whole life?
She and my father are always after me to cut my hair short.
They won't let me go out with girls. What do they know about
love? They don't even sleep in the same room any more. My
mother has such terrible headaches sometimes she is up all
night."

From Terry, and from his mother, I got a picture of his
father as a hard-working engineer, seldom home, who read
technical tomes when he was around the family. He had little
to say to his wife and son, though he seemed outwardly to love
the boy. Unfortunately, he disciplined his son at his wife's
whim.

The mother, I was forced to conclude, was a depressed
woman, burdened with physical ills, who said she loved her
son very much but seemed unable to show it except in a dominating, unconsciously cruel way. She kept repeating, "He'll
be the death of me, that boy, if he doesn't behave." She hinted
during a conversation that once she tried to commit suicide
with sleeping pills.

I had been seeing Terry three months (it was now summer and the trees in the park stood in full greenery) when he

said one day, "Mother and I had a fight last night. She didn't want me ever again to bring Charley Smith in the house. My best friend, Charley! She told me to tell him to stay away."

"What did you say?" I asked.

He blushed. Then he grinned, as happy an expression as I had seen cross his cherubic face.

"I told her to go to hell," said good, obedient Terry.

I could not help smiling. Terry was beginning to show some spirit. It was a healthy sign.

"What did your mother say?" I asked.

"She started to cry. She said I had no right to talk to her that way, that she was going to tell my father and I would get punished good."

"It was a strong thing to say to your mother," I remarked. "Even though I understand that you might want to say it."

His mother, of course, called to complain about her son's "mad" behavior. Now I was not his savior but the devil who allowed Terry to open his psychic Pandora's box.

"You've *got* to help him control himself," she stormed. "He's become impossible."

"Would you rather he starve to death?" I asked. (Some parents unconsciously would prefer this.)

There was silence at her end of the phone. Then she said, "What has one thing got to do with the other?"

"Terry has to learn to stand up for himself against you and his father," I told her. "Otherwise, he will become an emotional cripple. You have to let him make his own decisions about his personal appearance and choose his own friends." These are two of the main ways a child can learn to be independent.

It happens again and again that when a child gains sudden emotional strength, parents protest. Unconsciously they do not want the child to grow up. But if Terry had not found some way of releasing his rage, he would either have starved to death or, if persuaded to eat, might some day have physically attacked what he felt was an oppressive mother.

This is not to blame parents. Angry children have angry parents who were once angry children themselves but had nobody to help them.

Terry said to me one day, a few weeks later, "I hate my mother and I hate my father." He said it simply, earnestly, as though it were unassailably true.

"Tell them so," I said. "Tell them why you hate them. Tell them you love them, but at times you hate them for what they do to you."

He could not wait to report to me the following session. He said with joy, "I told them I hated them at times."

"What did they say?"

"They said I was sick in the head, even if I did eat my food now."

"Quite the contrary," I said. "You are much better. That is why you can tell them you hate them at times."

I talked at length with the mother and father, urging them to help Terry become independent rather than hinder his struggles to be free. His mother, a pretty, frail woman, came to see me and started to confess problems of her own with her husband, with whom she fought incessantly. (Scratch a troubled child and you find troubled parents.)

"Do you fight in front of Terry?" I asked.

She licked her lips nervously. "He's usually there when we fight. My husband picks fights at the supper table."

"Parents should try not to quarrel in front of their children," I said. "It upsets youngsters too much. Fight if you must—but not when Terry is around."

This may not be easy for parents to do, for when anger hangs in the air a spark of fury may set it off at any moment.

37

But it is well worth the effort, in terms of the child's psychic health, for parents to try to forgo the sadistic pleasure of quarreling in front of a child.

Here was a mother and father who fought openly, yet demanded that their son be well behaved. "Do as I say, not as I do," they were telling him. Such inconsistency is reason for rebellion in any boy or girl. Terry had tried to be a model of deportment, but sooner or later his pretense was bound to be exposed as false in any situation where there was psychic pressure.

Every youngster has a natural tendency to grow to maturity. He needs help in this growth, but help of the wise, compassionate kind, not punitive and restrictive. The latter will keep him forever a dependent, angry child.

Terry's parents tried to control him excessively, his mother and father acting as a unit. They approved when he was obedient and subservient to their wishes, but disapproved when he showed the least sign of fighting for his own identity. His mother, unconsciously, showed at times that she even resented his being born by telling him she had "given up so much" to take care of him and feed him, as though her life would have been far happier without him.

If Terry had not heard his mother say she would rather have his uncle dead than insane, if over the years he had not been so dominated by her that anything she said he automatically assumed to be the truth, he could have dismissed the priest's unrealistic warning. It was a combination of many experiences in Terry's life that led to the fear his mother would poison him.

It has been three years since I last heard from Terry after seeing him for a year. I assume all goes well and that his parents have learned how to permit him the degree of independence he needs to become an emotionally secure young man, capable of making up his own mind, accepting that sometimes he will be happy and at other times, unhappy, in his own choices.

I cannot urge parents too strongly to allow their children to grow up. Some parents resist their children's struggle to become independent, perhaps without even knowing what a battle they are waging.

A fifteen-year-old boy was sent to me because he was uncontrollably rude to his mother.

"Why are you so rude to her?" I asked.

"Why doesn't she let me grow up?" he demanded.

"What do you mean?"

"She bursts into my room at night when I'm studying or reading and she coos, 'You're my little baby, aren't you?' and I feel like vomiting. Why can't she talk to me intelligently?"

"But that's no reason to be rude to her."

He said pleadingly, "Doctor, *you* wouldn't want me to be *your* baby, at my age, would you? I was a baby long enough. That baby stuff kills me."

He was right, of course, even though it did not justify the way he talked to his mother and even though she provoked it.

I was lucky in that my parents allowed me to set my own pace of growth, although I occasionally had to fight for my independence. I felt particular empathy toward Terry because my oldest sister died in infancy and when I came along, three years later, I was overly protected. I might have been an angry child if I had not, at the age of seven, been able to fend for myself, to talk to both my parents when I felt they were not allowing me enough freedom.

One day I told them, "I want to be a big girl. I want to

39

ride on a train alone," and they allowed me to do so. I once said to myself, "Mommy is afraid of everything—even shadows. I don't want to be afraid of shadows."

Another time, when I was twelve, I left the house against their wishes to play tennis with some boys, and then again, to ride a bicycle into the country near Düsseldorf, in Germany, where I grew up. One day they followed me in the car and punished me with house arrest. They restricted me to our home after school and forbade me to play tennis with my friends for a few weeks.

I rebelled, saying, "I love you dearly but I will wind up hating you if you don't trust me."

From that time on, they did trust me—with myself, with money, with selecting my own clothes, for even as a little girl I had firm ideas as to what kind of dresses I liked.

My parents could have destroyed me if I had not possessed the spirit to resist them. When I spoke up, they understood my plea. As I recalled this, during my own personal psychoanalysis, I felt great gratitude toward them. I blessed them for their understanding of a little girl's desire to become an emotionally strong young woman. If they disagreed on a certain course for me, they talked it over with me, giving both their views and asking mine. They let me feel I was in on the decision.

As far as material things went, I was not given anything that was ostentatious or luxurious. If I wanted a special luxury, I had to earn it. I was made to feel I was no better off than the neighbor's child, whose father might be a city employee with a limited income. My father had gone to Germany when I was a baby to start a business there, taking his family with him. My grandparents on both sides were born in America. My mother's family lived in Georgia, and my father's, in Illinois.

My parents, as I grew up in Germany, did much to build up my ego—it was so strong that it came out the chimney, so to speak. I was always convinced I could do anything, meet any challenge. I was a young person with many interests. I learned to play professional tennis (once having as my partner the famed Bill Tilden). I learned to play the piano, the flute, to swim, to row a boat, to dance ballet professionally (teaching it for a while), even to fly glider planes until my parents made me give it up when my plane crashed.

My mother and father seldom fought, and if they did, never in my presence. They showed harmony and affection for each other in front of me.

I became a doctor at the suggestion of my father, although I wanted to be in some sports activity. He thought the sports world not a very satisfactory one for a woman. I attended Bonn University, in Bonn, Germany, then interned at Bonn University Hospital and Hôpital Cantonal de Genève, in Geneva, Switzerland.

Then I went to the United States, where I had always wanted to live, and began my professional life as a dermatologist in Santa Fe, New Mexico. In a short time, I developed a very active private practice. Patients would fly in from Denver, Colorado, and from cities located in states as far away as Texas and California (my patients included a number of well-known cinema actresses from the latter state).

It wasn't long before I discovered that numerous men and women who came for treatment of skin conditions also were suffering from emotional problems which, in many cases, had a direct relationship to the skin eruptions. A number of skin diseases were proven psychosomatic in origin, and other diseases were found in patients with serious mental disorders. This aroused my interest in psychiatry.

I left Santa Fe for New York City, where I studied and

41

worked for three years as a resident physician in the Bellevue Psychiatric Hospital of New York University. I was a full-fledged neuropsychiatrist at the end of my residency at Bellevue Hospital. In pursuit of a psychoanalytic career, I chose my own analyst from a list of names given to me. I interviewed all those on the list, then made as my choice a man who was one of the outstanding psychiatrists and psychoanalysts in America. As it turned out, he proved to be a great teacher, which helped me immeasurably in my practice. His parting words, incidentally, at the end of my analysis were: "You have a great instinct and intuition for helping people, important assets for your work."

Before I chose this man to be my analyst, one of the analysts who interviewed me asked why I was going into analysis. I replied, "Because it is part of my training."

"Unless you bring out your personal conflicts—conflicts that everyone has, bar none—unless you become aware of these conflicts and learn to deal with them, you will never understand the emotional suffering of your patients," he told me.

He was so right. During my analysis I found that I had problems of which I was unaware. For instance, I could never say "no" to a clerk in a store. I would walk into a shoe store, for instance, to buy a pair of white shoes. They would have no suitable white ones but I would walk out with a pair of black patent leather shoes under my arm because the clerk thought I should buy them.

As a result of analysis, I gained enough security to use that small, but very important word "no," at the right time in the right place.

The three hundred hours required as a minimum for analytic training helped me understand myself and helped me understand others, children and adults. After two years of

42

comprehensive training in psychoanalysis, I was certified as a medical psychoanalyst by New York Medical College, and have been in private practice ever since.

Psychiatry to me is the most rewarding of professions. Whoever has relieved emotional pain will know that because of its intensity and complexity it cannot be cured by pills alone. Sometimes a friendly word may be effective but often one must work patiently over a long period of time to ease emotional pain.

4.
SEX
REARS ITS
REALISTIC HEAD

ADOLESCENCE IS A TIME WHEN SEXUAL DESIRE, DORMANT
since the age of five or six, suddenly emerges with intensity.
In ancient times, and even in some primitive tribes today, at
the age of fourteen or fifteen it is natural for young boys and
girls to marry.

Part of nature's way of making sure the human race con-
tinues on its merry and sometimes unmerry way, is to ensure
there will be passionate feelings for members of the opposite
sex during adolescence. Civilization with its discontents and
stresses has postponed the marrying age. But normal, natural
sexual desire is still there and must be coped with somehow
by our young people.

If parents do not understand that it is normal and desirable for a boy or girl in their teens to be interested in love,
the parents may unconsciously hurt the youngster.

This happened to one boy, referred to me by his family
physician. At the age of eighteen Ben had gone to his doctor
to ask him to explain "the facts of life." The physician, aston-
ished, said, "Haven't you learned them from your friends?"
Ben confessed he had never discussed sexual matters, that he
was too shy to bring them up and his friends never talked
of sex in front of him.

"What about your mother and father?" the physician asked.

"Never mentioned it to them, nor they to me," he said.

The physician then explained "the facts of life" in scientific manner to Ben but noted that the youth appeared very anxious afterward. He suggested that Ben consult me to talk further about his feelings. Ben called and made an appointment.

He was a tall young man with a clean-cut face, very intelligent and serious, but shy and inhibited when the subject of sex or love was brought up.

"I can't talk about what the guys call making out," he admitted, "although I am very interested in getting married and raising a family after I'm through college." He was a freshman at Columbia University.

Then he laughed in an embarrassed fashion and said, "It seems funny to say this, but I have the feeling I am very angry at my parents for not telling me about sex when I was younger. Now that I'm grown up, it's too embarrassing to speak of it." (And the thought went through my mind that a girl of thirteen, who had been sitting in that same seat the week before, asked me, after she first masturbated, "Could I be pregnant?" and I had to explain to her how children are conceived and born, wondering why her mother never told her.)

Ben's father was a wealthy banker who took Ben, an only child, boating, golfing, and to country club parties. Ben also attended all the coming-out balls, making, I envisioned, a very handsome escort for any debutante. He was gallant, courteous, and trained in manners as if he had gone to West Point.

He respected his parents, he said, and thus was afraid to speak of "dirty things" in front of them.

"Sex isn't dirty," I said. "Sex is part of love, the most pleasurable feeling in the world."

"But my parents treat sex as though it *were* dirty," he said. "Whenever they tell an off-color joke, they send me to the kitchen for cold water for the drinks."

Ben was feeling the natural impulse to make love but did not know what to do about it. The urge to experiment sexually was driving him, yet at the same time he felt there was something wrong about giving in to it. The physician had thought otherwise, for he urged Ben to go out with his friends when they had dates, and hinted that perhaps he should visit a call girl.

Ben confessed to me that first session, "After seeing the doctor, I talked to my best friend, Jimmy, and told him what the doctor said. Jimmy not only gave me the address of a 'house' but took me there himself."

He described how Jimmy and he had taxied to a very elegant "mansion" in the East Eighties, a well-known brothel later raided and put out of business. When they arrived, they were separated and each was taken to a different waiting room.

"Every throw is fifty dollars," the madam told Ben. Twenty girls paraded before him so he could make his choice.

"My face changed from red to white, white to purple," he admitted to me, "as the girls marched in front of me. All I wanted was for someone to dash in and rescue me."

He reluctantly chose a girl who seemed as shy as he. She looked about fifteen years old and scared to death.

They crept upstairs to a small room, lushly furnished in keeping with the rest of the building, which held a kingsize bed. No sooner did she shut the door than the girl burst into tears. She was even more frightened than he.

She told him her name was Natalie, that she was just eighteen and had run away from home. Her father was a prominent physician, her mother a society matron. She felt her parents did not care what she did so she started going with

46

a group of "fast" girls in school. They led her to this "house" where they sometimes worked to make money.

"Where do your parents think you are?" Ben asked.

"I told them I was staying with a friend for several days. They really don't care what I do as long as I stay out of their way," she declared.

Instead of indulging in a sex orgy, the two spent half an hour talking. She confessed she thought she would be "fired" because in the week she had been there, no man had picked her out of the "line." She did not appear aggressive enough to be chosen; she was wearing her heart on her sleeve, so to speak. Unconsciously she was telling everyone she did not want commercial sex.

At the end of the allotted half hour, they went downstairs. He gave the madam $100, saying, "This is for two throws." He asked Natalie to meet him for supper the following night. She promised somehow to get away from the "house," which she did. This had been the night before our session.

Ben now asked me, "Was that the right thing to do? I want to help her."

"It was a gallant thing to do," I said. "Why don't you encourage her to leave that place, where she obviously does not belong, return home and get treatment."

"Would you see her?" His voice was eager.

"I'd be glad to." I felt sorry for these two troubled young people, victims of their confused feelings, not knowing where to turn.

Ben told Natalie what I had said. She called for an appointment. When she walked in, I saw a beautiful, shapely, dark-haired girl, with teary, large brown eyes, and a very shy manner. Next to her Ben seemed like a Napoleon.

Speaking on the verge of tears, she told me she felt unwanted in her home, that she adored her father but never saw

47

him because he was so busy with patients. Her mother was devoted to him and completely involved with social activities, so that she had little time for her daughter, an only child.

I suggested Natalie call her parents who, I suspected, were worried. She was afraid to speak to them, so I telephoned her father and told him his daughter had landed in my office. He asked to speak to her and requested that she come home, which she did. She did not tell her parents then about her week in the whorehouse. When she finally did confess to them, they were stricken but understood how, out of her desperation, she resorted to such an act. She reassured them that, while there, she had had no sexual relations and might just as well have been in a convent.

Ben and Natalie came to me for help for two years, during which time she started college. When Ben was graduated, they were married, having gone with each other ever since they had met in the brothel. This is a "truth is stranger than fiction" story.

When I asked Natalie, "What made you go into a whorehouse?" she replied, "I felt alone. At least there, I thought I would feel wanted."

"Sexually wanted, perhaps, but not wanted in a tender way, a way that would make you feel loved as a woman," I pointed out.

Many young people mistake sex for love. Sex is part of love, but other ingredients are equally as important, although at the age of sixteen or seventeen, they may not seem so. There is respect. There is friendship. There is admiration. There is compassion. There is understanding of the other person's struggles to survive, and of his defenses. There is recognition of how much tolerance he possesses and how much he is willing to share.

Ben's parents never discussed with him his feelings and

fears about sex but treated it rather as a "dirty, obscene" subject about which his innocent ears must not hear, sending him off on the silly excuse of getting "cold water" for their drinks (symbolically dashing cold water on any aroused emotion he might have at that moment when they were titillating each other with dirty jokes).

The controversial question as to how much parents should tell children about sex has occupied much space in our newspapers and magazines these past years. Some experts think sexual education should be left entirely to the schools. Others believe parents have the first obligation. Still others believe both parent and the school should share the task of helping the child acquire knowledge of sex.

There is nothing about which a child possesses more curiosity than sex. And there is probably nothing more difficult for a parent to talk to a child about than sex.

So many taboos and fears are associated with sexual behavior that it is perfectly natural that a parent should find himself speechless or anxious when his child first asks, "Where do I come from?"

At the same time, parents must realize that the best way to help a child grow up with a healthy approach to sex is to avoid being secretive about it, and not to treat it as a dirty crime. Since today's youth have available to them more information and are exposed to more sexual stimuli than ever, it is helpful to them to obtain information that will build in them a reasonable attitude toward sexual matters.

It probably is not so important *what* the parent says but *how* he says it. He can go into as many or as few details as he wishes in a calm, unanxious voice and the child will feel calm and unanxious. Or the parent can speak in a worried, anxious manner and the child will assume there is something worrisome and anxiety-provoking about sex.

49

Most important is the way parents behave toward each other in front of the child. If they are loving and tender, this feeling will be absorbed by the child. If they are hateful to each other, the child will sense this and it will distort his fantasies of love.

I should explain what "fantasy" means. There are two kinds of fantasy—conscious fantasy and unconscious fantasy. Conscious fantasy is comprised of our daydreams. A girl walks along the street dreaming of the handsome, successful man she will someday meet and marry. That is conscious fantasy. Or a youngster thinks how satisfactory it would be to get revenge on the English teacher who has flunked him, and imagines ways to humiliate her.

Unconscious fantasy is fantasy of which we are not aware but which influences what we do and feel. It flows from the unconscious part of the mind which, according to psychoanalysts, is the most powerful part. The conscious is only the top of the iceberg showing above the water, so to speak.

The unconscious is the storehouse of our memories as well as being responsible for directing the functions of our body, such as breathing, digesting, the beat of our heart. If we had to be conscious of every breath, every heartbeat, we would have no time to think or act.

Unconscious fantasy is often based on those wishes which, as a child, were too dangerous to think about for more than a second consciously, if at all.

For instance, a little girl upon viewing the naked body of her younger brother may wish she, too, had been born with the fancy appendage he possesses. However, feeling guilty about such a wish, she dismisses it from her mind. If the wish is very intense (if she is a very angry little girl), it may unconsciously dominate her later life as she becomes a driving career woman in a masculine world of work, or what is called

50

a "castrating female" in her home. Not all women who have the wish to be a man are found in careers. Many a housewife is equally as competitive with men.

Or a little boy may feel consuming jealousy over the new baby in the house and, for a moment, think, "I wish she were dead." He then feels guilty and tries forever to forget the wish. But if it is too intense (if he is a very angry little boy), he may have difficulty in later life overcoming his jealousy of women.

The "wish" is so important to psychic life because it is the wish upon which we act. The wish sets our body in motion. We cannot do one single thing without first wishing to do so. We feel hungry, so we wish to eat, and we eat, carrying out the wish. We feel affectionate toward someone, wish to kiss them, and kiss them, acting on our wish.

These are simple wishes. But there are wishes dangerous to our very life (a child may wish to murder—have the fantasy of murder—a parent who has punished him) and these are quickly relegated to the unconscious. The emotionally healthy child, suppressing such a wish, is not influenced by it. But the child filled with hate may find his behavior affected by the wish because of its intensity. And it may one day explode in destructive behavior. The boy who tears up his textbook in a temper tantrum, or the girl who barricades herself in her room and refuses to go to school, is overwhelmed by some unconscious fantasy or fantasies, so powerful they interfere with rational living.

Fantasies are the psychic accompaniment of a physical urge; they go hand in hand as mind and body respond as one to a stimuli. We feel hungry—the body is telling us to feed it so we can survive—and if food is available, we eat. But if no food is available, the next best thing for the moment is to imagine what a steak would taste like, to have the fantasy of a steak suddenly appearing to appease our hunger.

51

Unconscious fantasy is often related, thus, to an unful-filled wish. We do not get the wish, but we dream we do. Since the wishes most denied us have to do with hate—the wish to murder those we believe harm us—and love—the wish to fulfill our every sexual desire—it is logical that most unconscious fantasies whirl about sexual and aggressive needs.

Children have many fantasies about sex—where babies come from, what Daddy and Mother do in bed at night, what they look like naked. No matter what the age of the child, or young person, a parent should try to answer his questions honestly. A child will use just as much of the information he receives as he is able to understand. Some facts may go over his head. Then, at a future date he will again ask the parent, this time understanding.

One five-year-old girl asked her fourteen-year-old brother to tell her what happened between man and woman that produced a baby. He explained scientifically how a man inserted his penis into the woman's vagina.

The little girl remarked in wonder, "But doesn't that tickle?"

At her age, tickling represented the height of sexual intimacy. (Parents who tickle children, please note.)

If a parent is frank and sympathetic with the child's quest for knowledge about what is one of the strongest desires we possess, he will instill in the child the feeling that the sexual drive is natural, that it is a drive not to be ashamed of, but one to be controlled.

Civilization is built on the sublimation of our sexual and aggressive drives. Unless we want to live as in jungle days, we must learn to control these two drives. Children have to be taught to *want* to control them. If they do not learn this, they will grow up into cruel, selfish, greedy, wanton, undisciplined adults.

52

The danger is that some parents, in a desperate attempt to help the child control his dangerous urges, go to an extreme and overcontrol him. Or else, at the other extreme, they do not teach him enough control.

Either extreme will hurt the child. He must be *guided,* rather than *instructed* or *commanded* or *controlled* or *left to his own resources.*

Too little control was the problem of a mother who brought her son to Bellevue Hospital when I was a resident psychiatrist there. This mother (I never knew her name) came with her fifteen-year-old son to the mental hygiene clinic where I was fulfilling my assignment.

As I walked to my office one morning, I saw on a bench in front of the door this mother and her son, a head taller than she. They were waiting to see the psychiatrist in the office next to me, who had not yet arrived.

About ten minutes later, as I sat at my desk, I heard the other psychiatrist come into his office to get ready for his interview with the boy and his mother. The boy suddenly stood up and punched his mother in the head.

At this moment I opened the door to call in my first patient of the day. The mother, in fear, dashed through the open door, then closed it in protection, begging, "Doctor, please help me! I can't control my son. He's going wild."

The next thing I knew, the top half of my door, which was glass, shattered in a thousand splinters as the boy's fist crashed through it. He stalked into my room, took his mother by the throat and hair and tossed her into the hall. Then he walked to a steel cabinet filled with my files and hurled it to the floor so fiercely that it bent in several places. He overturned my oak desk, then pulled the telephone wire out of the wall. Luckily he left me unharmed.

Attendants rushed in and carried him off. I saw him in

the ward several days later. He remembered me and half-apologized, saying, "I don't know why I did what I did. I felt you were all out to get me. I lost control."

He had been in a fury because his mother rushed to me for help when she could not control him. Without knowing any of the facts, it is difficult to interpret the relationship between any mother and son. But here it was obvious that this young man of fifteen was struggling against powerful sexual and aggressive urges he could not control and was screaming for help in a defiant way.

He seemed also to be suffering from what psychiatrists call "paranoia." He was overly suspicious of everyone's motives and believed everyone was out to harm him. The anger of the paranoid may become so intense that he will commit murder as a result of his distorted fantasies. This boy had wrecked my room because he was suspicious of what his mother might be doing behind his back. His paranoia gave him superhuman strength, evident in the shambles he made of my office.

Another boy, whom I treated in my private office after I became a full-fledged psychiatrist, had received little aid in handling his sexual feelings.

Jimmy was one of eight children, next to the oldest, in a family where both mother and father worked to earn enough to pay rent and supply food for the children who sometimes did not get enough to eat.

When Jimmy was fifteen, he decided to help out his parents by working after school. He set up a small shoeshine stand on a street near where he lived. One day, while shining the shoes of an older man, he was surprised to be invited to the man's apartment and promised "a good steak."

Not knowing there was an unspoken bargain, he accompanied the man to his home. The man started to seduce him.

54

Because Jimmy was hungry, and because he was also sexually stimulated, he agreed to the seduction. He received the steak and also money, a sum that overwhelmed him.

He hurried home, gave his mother the money for food and said he had made it shining shoes. She rewarded him with high praise and a warm hug.

About once a week the older man would walk over to Jimmy's shoeshine stand and invite him to the apartment and he would go. Then he started to think, "Why can't I do this with other men and earn even more money?"

So, while he was shining shoes, if a customer seemed warm and friendly, Jimmy would slide his little fingers slowly up the man's legs in invitation to sex. Sometimes the man would respond and invite Jimmy for a brief sexual interlude, then toss him a few dollars.

How did a poor boy like this get into psychiatric treatment? Life is sometimes very strange. The man who originally seduced Jimmy became alarmed when he learned his sexual protégé had turned into a little "hustler." This man consulted his doctor, saying he had a young friend who was "all mixed up sexually." The doctor called me and asked if I would treat the boy. And as Jimmy's trust in and respect for me grew, he was able to abandon a way of life which he realized was destructive.

Someone else first must care in order that a child or young person can care about himself. Jimmy's mother and father had no time to care. Perhaps, too, they were emotionally unable to attend to eight children. Because of the youth's confidence in me, he was able to relive earlier, damaging experiences in his home, when he felt rejected as he saw one baby after another replace him at his mother's breast. I became a sympathetic mother figure who was trying to understand him, not the neurotic mother with whom he had to deal at home.

55

I always try to meet the mother of a child or youngster unless the latter is strongly opposed to such a meeting. I need to know how much the child's hatred is founded on fact, how much on fiction.

Sometimes a youngster will say, "Doctor, you won't *believe* what I go through with my mother. You've got to meet her to know what a monster she is."

Some parents *are* monsters. But sometimes I find the mother an outwardly sweet, helpless woman unable to control a child who has projected his own "monstrous" feelings on her. Sometimes he even sees his mother as an actual monster in a dream.

One fourteen-year-old girl in her dreams was always pursued by snakes. In one dream her mother turned into a snake. We talked about what "snake" meant to her. There is certainly nothing charming about a snake. It is a slithery reptile that sneaks up on you intent on biting you and it may kill you if its bite is poisonous. You have no way to fight it off. Its eyes mesmerize you. Most of us feel completely helpless in the presence of a snake. We fear it as we would an armed human enemy. Through the ages, the snake has also been a phallic symbol and, as such, creates additional fear. As far as this girl was concerned, the snake was symbolic of her mother. She actually feared and hated her mother.

Homosexuals are apt to consider their mothers "monsters" because in the fantasy of the homosexual "woman" is the enemy. The homosexual is a very angry young man. Homosexuality is a manifestation of hostility. The homosexual act is an act of anger. As a rule, it is an anal act and an aggressive act like rape, designed to let out hostility, not love.

I believe homosexuality can be cured, for this has happened several times in my practice. One twenty-seven-year-old man never had been able to love a woman. After three years

56

of treatment, he was able to marry and now has three children. The key to the successful treatment of a homosexual is the wish on his part to be cured. This includes his ability to look on homosexuality as an emotional illness from which he wishes to recover.

I have also treated lesbians. A nineteen-year-old girl came to see me and admitted she lived with another young woman whom she loved physically and emotionally. During her treatment she told me she wanted to give up loving a woman, marry and have children. This she did, after four years, and today is married and has two children.

Her father had died when she was five and her mother, who never remarried, often told her that men were to be hated and feared. Little girls whose mothers hate men absorb this feeling and hate men, too. Where there is too intense an attachment between a mother and her daughter, usually the mother wants the little girl all to herself and resents her being attracted to a man—the enemy.

The homosexual has a weak ego, in part the result of an overpowering mother to whom he has an overwhelming attachment, comprised of both love and hate. He is sucked into a subtle relationship with her, fulfilling in part her fantasies of a sweetheart. As a rule, the homosexual has an effeminate father, a silent bystander in the background, who gets sadistic pleasure out of the intensive love-hate displayed between mother and son. While the father may not be an acting-out homosexual, he usually is a latent homosexual who unconsciously is seducing his son, as his wife tears him down for not being a "man." When the son develops into a homosexual, the father, who usually has sexual problems, then gets sadistic pleasure out of watching his rival become impotent with women. I have never seen a homosexual who did not have as father "the sadistic observer."

57

Homosexuality for men, lesbianism for women, is part of the psychosexual development of all of us. The attraction for a member of the same sex is natural at a certain age, usually the early teens. The emotionally healthy young person will move on to the next psychosexual stage, when members of the opposite sex attract.

But if a child is too angry, too frightened of his parents and his own impulses towards them, he will not be able to move on to the next stage.

In children, we see sexual acts that appear to be miniature caricatures of adult perversions. Freud, in his analysis of five-year-old Hans, one of his famous cases, described the boy with the words, "Little Hans seems to be a positive paragon of all the vices."

Hans, an affectionate little boy, had suddenly been seized with a violent fear of horses. It was a fear so strong he would not go out into the street if a horse was in view. According to his father, who had been in analysis with Freud, Hans had been stimulated early in life by his mother's excessive display of affection and her too frequent readiness to caress him and take him into her bed.

"Lying in bed with his father or mother was a source of erotic feelings in Hans just as it is in every other child," Freud commented.

After hearing from the father at length about Hans's thoughts and behavior, Freud concluded that Hans feared that the horse—which symbolized his father, against whom he harbored jealous and hostile wishes—would bite off his penis because of his incestuous fantasies about his mother (a common fantasy among little boys).

His mother had warned him when she found him one night with his hand on his penis, "If you do that, I shall send for Dr. A. to cut off your widdler," the boy's word for his penis. But in spite of her threat, he fondled his genitals every night, telling his father frankly that he did so. With Freud's help, the father was able to allay the little boy's fears and his phobia about horses disappeared.

Before Freud, people believed children were little angels who never dared entertain a thought about anything as shameful as sex. Freud maintained that the sexual instinct is present, in both physical and psychological form, when we are born and that it gains power and maturity over the years. Our body grows and changes, sexually speaking, and so does our psyche.

Freud made the word "libido" famous. Libido means the psychic energy we put into our feelings of love, love of all kinds—for parents, for brothers and sisters, for the self, for members of the opposite sex, for friends, for humanity in general, even for specific objects like clothes or jewelry or stamp collections, or abstract ideas like democracy and freedom.

As a child we bestow the first signs of libido on our mother and father, the nearest and dearest people in our sphere of existence. But if for some reason a child is unable to do so, if he feels too rejected or guilty, his libido remains attached to himself. In later life he will be unable to love freely. This is what happens to the homosexual and lesbian, who seek as a sexual object someone whose body is fashioned like their own.

Children possess a sexual life that finds expression not only in sexual activities but also in sexual fantasies. These fantasies, even though disguised, revolve around the mother or father. Those who have cared for babies know how sensual they can be, how quickly they respond to the slightest loving touch. Among the Navaho Indians and other tribes, mothers sometimes stroke the genitals of angry babies to calm them down.

Freud theorized that our sexual functions undergo a complicated process in their development from the first erotic act of nursing at the breast, or being cuddled at the breast while fed a bottle, to the final stage of sexual intercourse. The sexual drive in a child is urgent and intense, and has a pleasurable quality, although the child is not capable of sexual orgasm. He wants sensual gratification, but only to the limited extent of his understanding of sex.

The essential difference between the adult and the infant is not that erotic wishes, hatred of rivals, and jealousy are absent in the earliest years, but that they are originally more intense, more specific, and less subject to immediate repression. This is pointed out by Dr. Ives Hendrick, psychoanalyst, in his classic book, *Facts and Theories of Psychoanalysis*. He says:

> For the child is too weak to avenge himself physically, and his sexual organs too undeveloped to accomplish more complete erotic satisfaction than that of masturbation, fantasy, and sexual games in secret with other children. But the passions are all the more intense at first, because he only gradually learns to bridle the emotional need of the moment in order to ensure more adequate satisfaction later on.

If an adult shows this kind of precipitous, unbridled emotion, unless there is exceptional provocation, he is seen as behaving in infantile fashion, Dr. Hendrick says.

What most adults prior to Freud failed completely to understand, maintains Dr. Hendrick, was the extraordinarily accurate intuitive powers of the child, who is "sensitive to emotional meaning, responds with exquisite accuracy to each change of feelings in those about him, even though they themselves are unaware of these deeper emotions."

This is so true of many emotionally disturbed children.

60

They pick up the feelings of their parents, both of love and hate, with, as Dr. Hendrick says, "exquisite accuracy."

Freud theorized that we all go through three important stages of what he called "psychosexuality." This is the psychic development that accompanies our body's sexual growth. These three stages are nature's way of preparing us to become fully matured sexually. They are normal stages which the average person passes through successfully. It is only in the angry child that each stage may possess an intense, distorted quality that may lead to weird fantasies and then to many forms of strange behavior.

The first psychosexual stage is the oral stage, when attention centers on our being fed and the pleasurable sensations of our mouth. This stage is divided into two parts: the sucking stage, and the biting stage when teeth form. In the baby's mind, the sexual instinct is not yet separate from eating, which is part of the instinct of self-preservation. The taking in of food, and the feeling of closeness with the body of the mother who gives food, are one and the same.

Sexual activity begins to develop apart from the process of eating when a baby begins to suck his thumb. He is trying to repeat the gratification he originally received from eating, by substituting a part of his own body for his mother's breast, or the nipple of a bottle, which he associates with her breast against which he lay as she fed him. Through the taste and feel of his thumb, he becomes aware of the pleasurable sensations he can get from a part of his own body.

The second psychosexual stage is the anal stage (both oral and anal stages are known as pregenital, in that the genitals have not as yet taken over as the main zone of sexuality). It is then we learn to control our bowels. We also discover a new kind of erotic pleasure with the holding back or giving forth of feces. We discover, too, our power over our parents.

61

We can either please them or make them furious if we do not obey their orders as to when and where to deliver our urination or defecation.

Excretions of the body are not unpleasant to children. At first, most children believe feces are precious parts of their own body that have become detached. Then they learn from parents to consider excretions disgusting and to feel embarrassment at the sight of them, the smell of them, and all noises that emanate from the bathroom. Some adults try to conceal the fact they ever go to the toilet because they feel so ashamed of what is a natural function.

During the anal stage we learn traits of cleanliness and order. If our toilet training is too rigid, in later life we may be overclean, overorderly, miserly, cruel, compulsive, or possess intense hatreds apparently without cause. Or in rebellion against a parent, some turn to slovenliness and disorder.

After the age of five, until the beginning of puberty, which may occur any time between the tenth and thirteenth year, sexual feelings lose urgency. This is known as the "latency period." The psyche gets a well-earned rest from the stresses of the strong childhood sexual urges. There now occur a few years in which we set up the defenses we will need for the beginning of puberty, with its very drastic psychic and physical changes.

Puberty is a time when the child may become rebellious and unruly as glandular and psychic changes prepare him for adult sexuality. The normal child discovers new outlets for his energies through sports, making friends, schoolwork, dancing, hobbies. At the end of puberty, he should be well on the way to becoming an independent being. He should be preparing to separate himself from his family (not that he can ever do this completely, for family ties are a desirable part of the rest of life, if they are comfortable ones).

During the third psychosexual stage, the genital stage, we reach sexual maturity. We feel free to express sexual love with one member of the opposite sex with whom we hope to live in intimacy, comfort, and harmony for the rest of our lives. By this time sex should have become a part of love, not a thing apart from it as during adolescence, when romantic illusions defend against the suddenly powerful genital sexual desires.

Turmoil is unavoidable in adolescence because the adolescent is "in physical and psychological limbo," says Dr. Rhoda Lorand, author of *Love, Sex and the Teenager,* and a psychologist who specializes in the psychoanalytic treatment of children and adolescents. She says:

> Literary evidence from all over the world and from every period of history attests to the fact that as a result of psychobiological tyranny, adolescence is a time of mental, emotional, spiritual, and physical upheaval, and therefore inevitably a time of anxiety. From the stable and fixed patterns of latency, the personality has suddenly become highly fluid. This allows for the reorganization and expansion of personality which takes place in adolescence—but it also leaves the adolescent worrying and wondering, "What am I really like?"

The world of romance and sexuality, heretofore experienced only in fantasy, she explains, suddenly looms as reality, bringing with it the question as to what extent the young person should respond. She calls this "an enticing, mysterious, alarming—and sometimes overwhelming—preoccupation, fraught as the sex drive is with dangerous consequences."

The awareness of parents as sexual beings must be dealt with before the adolescent can accept his own feelings as a sexual being. Dr. Lorand points out that "old Oedipal longings are revived and the adolescent wards them off, usually by flight from any involvement with parents, as a means of protecting himself against reexperiencing childhood attachments and desires. Feelings of rebellion and disdain serve as protection while, at the same time, giving rise to guilt feelings." But, she warns, this is the normal course of development. If it fails to happen, the young adult will remain in a childlike relationship to his parents (which, incidentally, a number of parents unconsciously wish their children to do).

In growing up, we all develop, to some extent, feelings of shame and disgust as one means of resistance against succumbing to our strong sexual urge. These feelings play an important part in helping us control our sexual feelings. But if they are too intense, or completely denied, they will distort how we feel about sex. We may feel shame and disgust to such a degree that we do not fully enjoy normal sex.

It is important to realize that children indulge in many fantasies appropriate to each psychosexual stage. The baby believes everything happens through the mouth, for that is the part of the body he knows best. During the anal stage, a child will have fantasies about the role of the rectum, imagining that babies, conceived through the mouth by the taking in of food (a fantasy carried from the oral stage), are born through the anus, for, as yet, the child is not aware of the function of the genitals.

We also go through three stages of love, Freud maintained. First, we love the self. Then, we love members of the same sex. Lastly, we love members of the opposite sex.

During the first stage, self-love, our own body is the object of our pleasure. During the second, the stage of homosexuality, we are attracted to the bodies of the same sex. In the final stage, heterosexuality, the bodies of the opposite sex are the object of love.

People who love only themselves are still babies emotionally. Narcissus, who fell in love with his own reflection in a pool of water, gave his name to a characteristic used to describe this first stage—narcissism.

The first stage, self-love, starts in the oral period when a baby discovers that his thumb will bring somewhat the same pleasure as his mother's breast or the nipple of the bottle. He next finds out that other parts of his body are sensitive and bring a pleasurable feeling if he touches or rubs them. This is desirable, for it leads to the last stage in sexual development, awareness of the genitals.

Most children before the age of four or five establish the genitals as the proper area for ultimate sexual functioning. They learn that a pleasurable sensation can be obtained by touching their genitals. Masturbation usually occurs at a later date, during puberty, when the child learns to reach orgasm or ejaculation.

The guilt most people suffer over masturbation is caused not by the fact that the act itself usually has been prohibited by word or look of parents, but because of the fantasies connected with it. These are primarily related, although they may be disguised, to the desire to love and be loved by the parent, a perfectly natural feeling.

Excessive masturbation, however, is a sign that a child is anxious or feels rejected. The child is saying, "Nobody loves me and so I will love myself." But parents should not, as some do, be curious as to whether a child is masturbating.

One eighteen-year-old boy who came to me for help at first would say only, "I hate my mother. She's too nosy." Weeks later, he explained further. "I remember that all during high school she would open the door of my bedroom at night when she thought I was sleeping and tiptoe over and pull off the blankets, to make sure my hand wasn't where it ought not to be," he said. "At first I was stunned by her little game, then horrified, then irritated."

Such a mother is unconsciously seducing her son. This kind of curiosity can only be attributed to her sexual interest in him.

Parents should not be alarmed when children find out that certain parts of their body give erotic pleasure. The stimulation by the child of these parts is a prelude to the building up of excitement in later years in parts of his body as the natural areas of forepleasure, adding immeasurably to the excitement in the act of love.

Because we have enjoyed pleasure from stimulating certain areas of our body as children, we become capable of greater pleasure in the adult sexual act, allowing ourselves to give forepleasure to another and to accept forepleasure from him. This means that sexual pleasure, which in childhood has been mainly concerned with the self, now can be directed partially toward someone else.

Love is a combination of sensuality and tenderness. Tenderness usually is learned during adolescence, although very sensitive children may acquire this trait earlier if they have parents who are tender toward them. If a parent is harsh and cruel, the child will have a difficult time feeling tender toward anyone later in life.

The indulgence in sex which hippies and other young people today flaunt as freedom is not the sex of love. It is masturbatory sex whose goal is the release of anxiety—originally caused by conflicts between parents and youth—by genital manipulation. There is little feeling for the other person as proved by the transitory nature of the relationships. It is as though "any penis" or "any vagina" will do for the moment.

Young people and adults may remain chained to a childhood level of sexuality if at an earlier stage of love or psycho-

sexual development they received either too much sexual pleasure (became so overstimulated they did not know how to
handle their aroused feelings) or too little pleasure (became so
frightened of their body they could accept no enjoyment from
it).

If a child feels he is "bad" when he masturbates (when
a child feels "bad," this is usually connected to masturbation)
and struggles against his natural desire to do so, prohibiting
himself from ever touching his genitals, his Oedipal fantasy is
thus denied an outlet. But the dammed-up sexual energy attached to the natural masturbatory impulse, and to the fantasy
as well (remember, each impulse is woven round with fantasies), will find its way out, perhaps in delinquency, perhaps in
withdrawal from reality, or compulsive behavior of some sort,
many times spurred by a conscious or unconscious hatred of
parents. Such a child is likely to sexualize everything out of all
proportion to reality. Denied an outlet, the sexual instinct may
overflow and submerge other parts of the personality.

I have seen little children seduced out of their wits by a
parent's overpowering sexual desire even though the parent
may do nothing more than hug or kiss them—but with great
hunger and intensity, as though the little child were a lover.
The nervous, tense, precocious little girl or boy who can never
be still, who must always be running, running, running, often
has a parent who somehow has overstimulated them sexually.

On the other side of the coin stands the parent who, because he feels his sexual urge to be evil, dares not even kiss or
hug the child. This child will grow up believing there is something sordid and evil about his own passionate feelings.

The parent who has control of his own emotions, who
truly loves the child, knows when to give affection and knows
enough to keep affection temperate. He does not need to use
the child as target for his own emotions.

67

A significant report was made recently by two California scientists. They revealed that the "information-processing" parts of the brain develop faster in animals that are handled, stroked, shaken, sung to, and otherwise stimulated during the first days of life. These findings suggest early life experiences can influence ability later in life, according to Dr. Shawn Schapiro, one of the scientists.

Evidence indicated that different types of sensory stimulation are necessary to insure a child's normal rate of development, said Dr. Schapiro, Chief of the Developmental Neuroendocrinology Laboratory at the Veterans Administration Hospital in San Fernando, California, and member of the psychiatry staff of the University of California at Los Angeles.

In his studies, litters of rats were removed from their nests three to five times a day and subjected to half an hour's stimulation. They were handled, stroked, and shaken on a mechanical shaker, placed in warm and cold water, on cold and warm metal, subjected to sounds, flashing lights, and electric shocks.

It was found that the stimulated animals had more brain nerve cells that took up a cell stain called Golgi stain. "This suggests that stimulation had increased the cells' functional level," explained Dr. Schapiro.

In applying these findings to human development, he said, "We don't know yet what kind and quality of sensory stimulation are optimal for brain development." He added that, in light of the findings, "It seems odd that in the United States and in many European cultures, the young child who stays in his own room and is quiet all day is considered desirable. It would seem that the child who is fully involved in the hubbub of family life, who is constantly being stimulated, would have the greatest chance of reaching his full potential."

The implications of this study to the psyche are important. It would appear that too much early physical stimulation, too much touching by parents, nurses, or other relatives of a child may make him precocious and brilliant, but also nervous and probably prone to emotional conflicts. A child will become furious when he can find no outlet for his early sexual arousal and will inevitably blame his parents. Early precocity appeared in the lives of many of our geniuses, indicating there may have been much stimulation of their senses by parents, siblings, or relatives in their early lives. In Freud's book, *Leonardo da Vinci, A Study in Psychosexuality,* he arrives at this theory.

Too little stimulation probably produces withdrawn, shy, lethargic children. The answer seems to be for parents to provide the child with a reasonable amount of sensory stimulation, just enough for the child to cope with comfortably.

If our psychic processes are interfered with too drastically as we grow up, we may not advance naturally from one sexual stage to the next. A boy with too deep an erotic attachment to his mother may never get beyond the homosexual stage. He may be unable to free himself emotionally enough to reach for another woman, even after he is physically and intellectually mature. He cannot tear himself away from his mother, psychically speaking. In effect, the homosexual gives up his penis, for he cannot use it to possess his mother. This is taboo. He can remain with her only if he sacrifices his masculinity. He looks for a man, a creature with a penis, to replace his own, in fantasy. This allows him to perpetuate the early love affair between his mother and himself.

Although the stages of the development of our love and sex life are biologically determined, their final outcome may be affected by how a parent reacts along the path of growth.

Too much frustration at any one of the three sexual stages may lead to later conflicts. If a child is treated harshly when

69

he is first fed or toilet-trained, or if during adolescence his parents make him feel sex is an evil, never to be indulged in, rather than a natural desire, to be controlled, it may be difficult for him to grow to sexual maturity.

Toilet training represents one of our first important frustrations. We are told we can no longer indulge in the pleasure of excreting whenever or wherever we please. We do not like this control over us. But we give up our strong wish to do as we like because we want the love of our parents. Without that, we could not survive.

From then on, whatever is anal becomes the symbol for much that is hated and condemned. It is no accident that the word "shit" in our culture carries the connotation of the utmost contempt and disgust. Yet toilet training is a necessity, for without it, not only would it be difficult to live with other men, but frustrations would be harder to accept. Parents who have been too indulgent, postponing training until a child is five or six years of age, will have an angry, irritable child on their hands, one who has trouble accepting any kind of frustration. It is no favor to a child not to train him at the proper time, between the ages of two and a half and three.

If a child is trained too early, before he is biologically able to handle control of his bladder and bowels, there will also be a very angry child. He may go through life hating his parents, never knowing why.

How parents feel about their own sexuality will influence a child's attitude towards his sexuality. If parents do not get along with each other sexually, the child will become aware of this and be confused about his own feelings.

A child's erotic feelings for his parents are accompanied by a psychic need for love, tenderness, and approval, and as he receives these, his self-esteem develops. If he does not get love, tenderness, and approval on a day-by-day basis, his erotic feelings are likely to be disturbed. And vice versa: When his erotic feelings are disturbed, that is, if he is overseduced or deprived of affection, his psychic needs will suffer, and hostility —conscious or unconscious—toward his parents will ensue.

The parent who does not understand the child's need for love, tenderness, and approval is likely to be the parent who will upset the child's emotional and erotic balance. This is the parent who beats the child, who screams at him endlessly, who fondles him excessively. Or one parent may do all three things, one moment striking the child, then screaming at him, then, guiltily, trying to make it up to him by passionate embrace.

Incidentally, it is unwise for a parent to allow a child to sleep in the same room, even when he is a tiny baby. Parents may not believe a baby is aware of what goes on, as they engage in making love right before his eyes, but a baby is extremely sensitive to noise, movements, and sounds. He may not know exactly what is happening as he witnesses or listens to his parents making love. But the impression it leaves on his mind is indelible. He is apt to retain the vision as something violent that befalls his mother at the hands of his father. A child's aggressive and sexual feelings are so fused that he interprets sexual activity as brutal, and the child may develop an unconscious hatred of the father who, he mistakenly believes, is beating his mother.

Our sexual feelings are so complicated that, when they become disturbed, they are apt to affect almost every area of our lives. But when they fit comfortably into daily living, when we feel in harmony with them, they add the greatest of pleasure and satisfaction to existence.

This is one thing youth has to find out for itself. No one can order an adolescent to postpone an instant pleasure that may hurt him, for a delayed, more satisfactory pleasure. He has to discover the reward of postponed pleasure for himself.

71

5.
THE
OEDIPUS
HANGUP

EACH TROUBLED ADOLESCENT SOONER OR LATER HAS TO FACE his feelings about the parent of the opposite sex. It is normal and natural for a child to experience yearning for the parent of the opposite sex. All little girls want to marry "Daddy" and all little boys want to marry "Mommy."

As he grows up, the child learns to sublimate this yearning. He transfers it to those his own age and puts some of the psychic energy bound up in this wish into studies, hobbies, and other activities.

But some adolescents are unable to accept their feelings for a parent as natural at one stage, to be given up at a later stage. They are unable to transfer their love to someone more appropriate, without experiencing tremendous pangs of guilt.

If a young person has gone through the earlier psychosexual stages fairly easily—which means he has felt loved—he will not have too much trouble accepting his Oedipal feelings. But if those earlier years held psychic trauma, he may face deep conflicts about the parent of the opposite sex.

One sixteen-year-old girl blithely informed me, as though daring me to do something about it, "I'm hung up on my Oedipal feelings for my father."

At least she was aware of it. But that was only the first

step. She had intellectual awareness, but not the emotional awareness in which one accepts the feelings in one's heart, blood, and bones, as well as in the mind. Emotional awareness develops during treatment while a patient is talking over various events of the past connected to his feelings and discovering deeper ramifications.

Where there exists deep yearning for one parent, there exists hatred of the other parent. The child naturally wishes the parent of the same sex were out of the way forever so he could be sole possessor of his beloved. Oedipus slew his father, not knowing his father was Laius, king of Thebes, whom he met on a lonely road. After the murder, Oedipus continued his journey from Corinth to Thebes, where he met Jocasta, widow of Laius, not knowing she was his mother. He fell in love with her, married her. Sophocles had to write of Oedipus as being unaware of the filial connection for it would have been too much to ask a reader in those pre-Freudian days to accept incest performed knowingly.

In *Hamlet,* Shakespeare tells of the tragedy of a son in love with his mother. But here the incestuous love is deeply repressed and never acted upon, beyond an ardent kiss. Hamlet's guilt, however, shows itself in his postponing his desire to avenge his father's death by killing the murderer, Hamlet's uncle Claudius who has married Hamlet's mother. Hamlet hesitates at the very moment of murder because he himself unconsciously wished to murder his father and possess his mother, according to an interpretation given by Ernest Jones, world-famous psychoanalyst. How can Hamlet kill a man for doing the horrible deed he himself longed to do? Is he not equally guilty?

Shakespeare summed it up with the line, "So conscience doth make cowards of us all." Our conscience is our guilt over a wish we repress as evil.

73

The deadly struggle that may take place between father and son was brought out in *The Golden Bough,* by Sir James George Fraser. This book illustrates in myths the symbolic killing of the father—the old man—by the son, his youthful successor. Fraser discovered in his study of primitive societies that the king, in many cases, was put to death by his people or took his own life, at the first sign of frailty. His subjects believed prosperity would wane, cattle fall sick, crops sink to ruins, and they themselves die of disease, if the king's virility failed.

Kings and presidents and high officials are slain today because, in part, they represent the hated father in the unconscious of the murderer (even when the motive may be consciously political or for a "cause"). For instance, Lee Harvey Oswald appears always to have selected a father substitute, according to testimony given by his wife. He shot at General Walker, then planned to kill Richard Nixon, and finally did kill "the father figure" of the nation.

Where taboos are most stringent, we find emotions most passionate. The taboo against incest is possibly the most powerful one we have. Thus we can take it for granted that the emotions revolving around the parent of the opposite sex are also the most powerful.

Savage tribes share a deep dread of incest. There is such strong prohibition against it among certain Australian tribes that should a man and woman dare break the taboo, they are both put to death. The entire tribe sits in judgment as though to ward off a danger and guilt feared by all. Among the Battas of Sumatra, a brother cannot take his sister to a party. Nor will a father stay in the house alone with his daughter, or a mother with her son. These tribes guard against possible incest, taking it for granted that if a man and woman are left alone sexual intimacy will result whether they are related or not.

Parents have to help a child weather the Oedipal storms. Some very disturbed parents are unable to do so. There are cases in children's courts of fathers who have seduced little daughters. More rare is the mother who seduces a son, although that happens, too. In a famous case several years ago involving a son who shot his mother, he was acquitted by the jury when it was revealed that his mother had seduced him at the age of twelve and had insisted he sleep in the same bed with her until he broke away and fell in love with a young woman his age and his mother threatened to kill him. The jury took into consideration the enormity of her crime in reaching the verdict.

The Oedipal conflict is one that faces us all and is solved most comfortably by those sons whose fathers have a good relationship with them, who understand what they are going through and are not contemptuous or cruel. The son then sees his father not as a castrative monster out to destroy a younger rival, but as a sympathetic parent who wants his son to become independent and manly. The daughter's relationship to her mother, if a good one, will insure that she gives up her yearning for her father.

If feelings for a parent of the opposite sex are overdramatized and overerotic, a young person will not be able to handle his Oedipal wishes successfully enough to accept their frustration and progress to more mature relationships.

Human beings go through a long time of helplessness. A child depends for years on his mother for survival. This is what Freud called "the human condition." If a mother is overprotective and overpossessive, it becomes difficult for a child to separate himself from her. If, on the other hand, a mother neglects a child, he will spend his life unconsciously hating her and psychically screaming for the love she failed to provide.

If a mother vacillates between the two extremes, neglecting her child one moment, indulging him wildly the next, his emotional development is also bound to be thwarted. Such a child lives in constant dread, never knowing what is expected of him. Children need consistency in affection and attention.

Nature, interested in the perpetuation of the species, intends children to break away from parents. A young person's choice of mate is based in part on his original love for his mother and father. But the more successful he is in separating himself emotionally and erotically from his parents, the more wisely will he be able to choose the person whom he wants to love for the rest of his life.

Freud pointed out that many sons have the fantasy their mother is a prostitute. This is caused, in part, by the desire of the son to possess his mother; he must then punish her for having sexual intimacy with his father—if she sleeps with his father, she must be a whore, for she is untrue to him, her son. Also, if she is a prostitute, then she really does not love his father, she only sleeps with him out of a sense of duty, sacrificing herself for the love of her son so she can bring him up with all advantages.

If a son does not give up this fantasy, he may consider every woman a whore. He may go from affair to affair, in which his apparent "love" for the mistress is actually a manifestation of hate, because his guilt over committing an incestuous act in fantasy is so great he must abandon each woman.

Most people work their way out of the Oedipal stage. No one ever completely frees himself of the idolatrous love for parents—seen as gods in childhood—but the emotionally healthy person accepts this feeling and does not let it interfere with his love for someone else.

If, as has been demonstrated by anthropological and psychoanalytic studies, the daily aura of living is a comfortable one, the child will weather anything that happens to him in later years. He learns how to use his feelings of both love and

76

hate in an appropriate manner. He will be able to pass success-fully through the Oedipal crisis.

Money and the Oedipal conflict may be related in a subtle, complicated way. If a son is afraid to make money, on an unconscious level it may mean he is afraid to compete with his father. Competition with the father means, uncon-sciously, competing for the love of the mother. Some sons have the fantasy that if they become more successful than their father in any way, this means they defeat him in the game of love, with the mother as stake. They come up against the Oedipal taboo which is associated with castration and death.

Most of us suppress our Oedipal feelings successfully, ex-cept for the schizophrenic who may talk of his longings in a way no other man would admit. For instance, the schizo-phrenic child sometimes speaks of feelings the normal child represses, such as the desire to sleep with the parent of the opposite sex. He may also describe in detail seeing his mother and father having intercourse when he was smaller and slept in a bed, or crib, in the same room. The more normal child will have buried these images. In Robert Lindner's book, *Rebel Without a Cause,* the young man who has committed a crime is taken back through the years under hypnosis, and recalls, as a baby, having been frightened to death when he saw his mother and father in the sexual act.

A nineteen-year-old youth walked into my office one morning for his first appointment. He was slim and handsome, with the All-American boy look. No sideburns or straggly beard for him. His blond hair was combed carefully back from forehead and ears, his face, clean-shaven.

"Hello." I put out my hand, as I always do the first time a patient enters my office.

He shook my hand firmly, asked, "Do I have to lie down on the couch?"

77

"Not if you don't want to." I wait until someone is ready to stretch out on the couch—until, if he has come to be analyzed, he realizes that only in this position is he likely to feel free enough to say everything that comes to mind. This young man had called and said he wanted "a deep analysis."

"I think I'll just sit in this chair for now." He lowered himself into the chair across from my desk. His manner was one of slight detachment, as though he were determined to be impersonal about what are essentially very personal matters.

"How did you happen to come to me?" I inquired.

"I got your name from a medical organization that supplied me with a list," he said. "I went down the list alphabetically. First I saw three male psychiatrists. Now you." He hesitated, then resumed. "I think I want to start treatment with you."

"Why?" My voice was gentle.

"There is something about you that resembles my mother," he said. "I feel at home here. Maybe it's the way you've decorated the room."

He looked around, his gaze settling on the window sill where the three monkeys—*See no Evil, Hear no Evil, Speak no Evil*—were perched.

"Isn't that a strange thing to find in a psychiatrist's office?" he asked. "Aren't patients *supposed* to speak evil?"

"Nothing is evil in this room," I told him.

His eyes returned to me. He said, "I borrowed enough money for six months of treatment. I hope I can solve my problems by then." The blue eyes were challenging.

"Tell me about yourself." He seemed an extraordinarily brilliant youth, sophisticated and wise beyond his age.

"I'm studying to be a stockbroker. I've been married about a year. I had to marry my wife because she got pregnant." He bit his lips, then retreated into silence.

78

I waited. He lit a cigarette and drew on it several times. Then, as though plunging into icy water, he confessed, "In this day and age, with everyone making out, it sounds ridiculous. But the only time my wife and I had sexual relations was when she got pregnant."

He went on, "Even more ridiculous is the fact that I never had sex before I married. Nor did she. We both were virgins, if you can believe it. We were really uptight. And the time we did make out, we both were very nervous. We found it difficult to get together in bed."

What a strange way to describe sex, I thought, "to get together in bed." As though the man and woman were enemies.

"I have financial problems, too," he admitted. "My father is a wealthy stockbroker. But I lose money. Every stock I pick goes down. I have a knack for selecting exactly those stocks that fail. I seem to know the very moment they're due to fall, and buy the day before."

"You're not like your father in that respect?" I asked.

"I hope I'm not like him in any respect," he replied heatedly.

"Why?"

"Because I hate him. He's a pompous, tyrannical bastard. He can't stand me, either. He always praises my younger brothers but tears me down."

"How many brothers do you have?"

"Three."

"You're the oldest of four boys, then." I could imagine some of the conflicts that arose in his life when he was a youngster.

"The house was always cluttered with kids screaming at each other as I grew up. I couldn't wait to get out of it." His face lost its handsomeness for the moment as his mouth and cheeks contorted in confusion. "I wouldn't go to college. I wanted to go right to work in the stock market. Dad took me into his firm and gave me money for a start. I promptly lost all of it."

He talked on, chiefly about his ventures in the market and how they always failed. He mentioned stocks familiar to me, since I had a few investments, and stocks of which I had never heard. The fifty minutes passed swiftly.

He stood up finally and said half jokingly, "Well, I'll come to see you for six months, which is all I can afford with my loan. If you can help me make money in the next six months, I'll stay another six."

"Fair enough." We shook hands.

He was back the next day for his second session. He told me about a fight with his wife who, he said, had refused the night before to make out with him, claiming she had a splitting headache. He became furious at this rejection and screamed at her.

"I called her a frigid bitch," he said, then added angrily, "She really is."

I listened as he stormed on. It did not seem difficult for him to vent his rage upon his wife. It was a different story, though, when it came to his mother. He idolized her. As he spoke of her, a soft look came into his eyes, as if he wanted to cry.

"Mother has put up with so much over the years," he said. "She has taken such abuse from my father. And her other sons, too. They all ride roughshod over her." He added defensively, "She knows she has her champion in me."

It was easy to see how he was transferring the anger he must have felt at times as a boy for his mother (because she betrayed him by having other sons and tolerated the father's abuse) to his wife, using *her* as the target of his *unreal* wrath.

He had never seen the "wife" in his wife, only the "mother," and the "bad mother" at that. His mother had remained in his fantasy only the "good mother."

I would not say this to him. He would discover it soon enough if he kept talking. I would point it out when I thought he was ready to hear it.

He started to visit regularly four times a week. At the end of the fifth week, as he entered my office, he said in too-casual a tone, "I think I'll lie down on the couch today."

"Fine." I took my place in the chair at the head of the couch, with its two large green and blue floral print pillows. There I could listen carefully and also observe those signs of the body that occasionally betray the patient's feelings.

"I guess I'll tell you a dream," he began.

Many patients who lie on the couch tell of their dreams. It is an excellent way to reach buried thoughts; Freud called it "the royal road to the unconscious." I was delighted that he wished to relate a dream—the first time he had mentioned one—since from dreams would flow valuable fantasies that would help him understand his conflicts.

"I dreamt last night—it's a dream that occurs often—I was playing baseball with a bunch of the boys in high school. I stood in center field and each time the ball was hit to me, I tried to catch it but would drop it. I would feel embarrassed as hell and want to die."

He was silent, not knowing what to say next. I suggested, "What does the dream make you think of?"

"Just what I do on the market," he replied eagerly. "I try to catch stocks as they go up, but all they do is drop—like I dropped the ball. And then I feel embarrassed and ashamed."

Something else in his life "dropped," too, instead of "going up," but I was not going to point that out yet. Psychiatrists learn not to make interpretations too quickly. As

81

André Gide wrote, "Do not understand me too quickly," and this applies to patients.

We may know, theoretically, what is going on, but to interpret too soon may mean arousing fear and hostility in someone you want to help overcome those emotions. Part of the art of therapy is intuitively estimating the exact moment to put forward an interpretation so the patient may use it. He may not use it at once, but he is ready to store it in his mind for use when he feels safer, rather than dismissing it as nonsense.

This young man found it easier to talk of his troubled reflections as he lay on the couch. He started to speak of his life as a boy, the oldest of four sons. He began to feel childhood anger at his mother for bearing three other children, and for having him first, thus making him suffer rejection three times.

His hidden anger at his mother and father had kept him from being assertive in his profession and as a man with a woman. He could shout and scream but he lacked true assertion, which needs no anger to propel it but is inspired by conviction. Assertion, to me, means a firm approach in a friendly manner to people and to work. Aggression is a hostile way of expressing oneself.

This young man was aware he had sexual problems. He knew that for him to have sexual relations with his wife once a year—the time she got pregnant—made him somewhat of a freak. He had deep fears about sex. He could not even acknowledge that conjugal relations took place between his mother and father. He wanted to deny it, as he had denied it in his own life. If we cannot grant that our parents are entitled to express sexual feelings, it is difficult to accept that the same privilege is our natural right.

"I guess my mother and father must have slept together —at least four times," he remarked sarcastically.

"Just as you slept with your wife once and a baby was born," I commented, thinking how strong fantasy can be, how it can influence behavior. This youth fantasied that his parents had had intercourse only four times—each time a baby was born. And this was exactly what he had done in his life, unconsciously caricaturing his parents.

He also recalled he had been "insanely jealous" of his brothers, especially the youngest whom he once had tried to hurt by striking him when he lay crying in his crib.

"I feel so guilty," he confessed. "I never told anyone about this before. I fled to my room sobbing. I knew I had done wrong even though no one saw me. Luckily, I didn't hit him hard."

As he talked about his work, he revealed his need to remain at the edge of poverty. As soon as he made money, he immediately spent it, so he could never catch up. He barely supported his wife and child as though begrudging them any money he earned. But he paid for and came regularly to his sessions. Six months passed, reaching the time he had indicated he would have to terminate treatment unless he had earned money.

On the very day that marked the end of six months, he walked into the room, smiling. It was the first smile I had seen cross his face.

"I have made twenty-five thousand dollars since coming here," he announced proudly. "I seem to pick the right stocks now. My father is willing to lend me money to go on with my treatment. He thinks something good must be happening here."

He was telling me he was getting enough out of the sessions so he could, at last, use his intelligence and the skills learned from his father, to invest more wisely.

With the ability to earn more money also went the ability to be more of a man. After months of tension and many false starts—apparent frigidity on the part of his wife and partial impotence on his part—he now seemed to enjoy sexual relations. It was not something to be dreaded or ignored. His wife no longer talked of headaches—a frequent and annoying complaint—and appeared more willing and cooperative. In other words, once he conquered his own sexual fears connected with his conflicts about his parents, he was able to approach his wife with more spontaneity and she, in turn, responded.

He came for treatment for two years and at the end of that time he had amassed almost $300,000 in the market. He had overcome his sexual inhibitions so that he and his wife enjoyed regular intimacy. He realized one of his fears about sex was that he believed that each time he made love a baby would be born. This had awakened the terror he felt as a child when he saw his mother become pregnant again, three times.

On the last day I saw this young man, he talked of a dream reminiscent of the first one he had described, but with one great difference.

"I was playing pool," he said. "Suddenly the pool table turned to a roulette wheel and the balls turned into dice. Then the dice turned into money."

He associated to the dream: "Pool table—roulette wheel —gambling—Wall Street, where I make money. I no longer drop the balls in panic. I turn them into dice, something to be used and enjoyed."

His dream revealed the wish to make money and the wish to enjoy his masculinity. As he said, "balls" were no longer a plaything he dropped "in panic" but were to be used for pleasure.

He was no longer so afraid of his father. He could accept both his father and mother as human beings rather than the stalking giants of childhood who had once frightened him to death and had been the triggering mechanism of hostility and rage. He was finally ready to become a father himself.

Incidentally, I did homework for this case. My bedtime and before-breakfast reading became *The Wall Street Journal* and reports of various companies on the exchanges. Although I owned stocks, I had never shown much interest in them. Now I realized how much fun it was to keep track of the market. This helped me tremendously, as I started to see a number of brokers as patients I found myself able to comprehend what they were talking about. I believe in getting a picture of the patient's whole world—his career and practical needs as well as his psychic needs. If I had a jockey on the couch, I would read the *Morning Telegraph*. I read *Woman's Wear Daily* for my models and designers.

But not only for models and designers do I read about fashion. I do so because of all my patients. I take special care in how I dress.

I have never forgotten that when I attended medical school at Bonn University, the professor of anatomy, a world-wide authority, author of a three-volume classic in anatomy, told his women medical students: "You cannot be sloppy in the way you dress. If you want to be a doctor, you have to dress better than your patients. They have to look up to you and respect you for how you look, for that tells what you think of yourself. It is an indication of your trust and confidence in your own skill."

In my practice as a psychiatrist, I have learned that patients must be able to consider their doctor, sartorially speaking, as the highest example of dignity and chic. Many times I have thought of the wisdom of my anatomy professor who consistently called our attention to the importance of not only being earnest (on time and reliable in the promises we made) but well-dressed.

The value of appropriate dress was driven home by a patient who was a businessman. He told me one day, "I don't feel good looking at you in your red dress. I have problems and staring at red doesn't help me solve them. Red radiates some kind of mood adverse to how I want to feel, if I have to face my conflicts."

At his next appointment I wore a green dress. In a polite manner, he spoke up again. "I should feel comfortable now that you're not wearing red. But green is a color I also dislike intensely." He had traveled all over the world, including France, and he mentioned that the French had a superstition that green brought bad luck, which, he said, was why Frenchmen would not wear green ties.

After he left, I wondered what to wear for his next session and decided pastel colors would be best. In this assumption I proved to be correct. Eventually, we discussed why the colors red and green disturbed him. Red to him symbolized "blood," which he could not stand, and "green" stood for envy, the "green-eyed monster." This was a man with great anger at his parents and intense jealousy of a younger sister.

Another patient suffered from mystagmus, a physical condition in which the eyes have difficulty focusing. I was wearing a print dress which, he said, bothered him so intensely he developed a headache because of the disturbance to his vision. So prints were out for this patient. When I saw him, I wore only plain colors.

Many a youthful patient comments on the color or style

of my clothes because almost every child is conscious of what his mother wears. One woman told me that the light blue of a dress was a cool color, reminding her of the sea. She recalled that her mother always dressed her in blue to match her eyes. Since I was to her the "punitive" mother at that point in her treatment, I did not wear blue for her sessions.

It is important to please patients if they dislike certain aspects of my dress (always later to examine why they dislike that particular color or style). They should feel comfortable and safe, not hostile and prone to make unpleasant associations to the therapist. None of them like me to wear black— they feel it is depressing, reminding them of funerals and death. You cannot antagonize a patient esthetically and expect him to trust you with his innermost secrets. That is why I will never wear a color to which a patient reacts negatively.

Also, I think it is most important how the analyst looks because the patient, especially the depressed adolescent or adult, will not care how *he* looks if he faces a dowdy analyst, with whom he is bound to identify, both consciously and unconsciously. Several girls have told me that, after sessions with me, they feel inspired to go home and put on prettier dresses and matching accessories.

I have learned much from my patients as, over the years, they pour out their innermost secrets, secrets of which they have been ashamed but which, hopefully, they no longer will fear as they air them in the light of reality.

6.
THE
ANGRIEST
YOUTH OF ALL

IF EVER A CHILDHOOD CONTAINED ALL THE CLASSIC PSYCHO-
logical elements destined to create anger so devastating it
erupted in murder, it is that of the man charged with master-
minding what some authorities have labeled "the crime of the
century," and of the twenty-one-year-old girl who turned him
in. This man drew into his orbit of horror a number of equally
furious teen-agers.

I shall go into detail about what we know of the lives of
the teen-agers involved, and the man himself, because I feel
it is important to understand the extremes in human behavior.
The extremes act as a magnifying glass so we can see clearly
what may hurt a child so deeply that he vows undying revenge
on those who brought him up, often taking this revenge, however, on the innocent who only symbolically represent his
parents.

If we can understand the reasons for murder in the heart
of a murderer, we can understand the reasons for anger in the
heart of a child who at times feels murderous.

A shocked nation read on August 10, 1969, in its Sunday
morning newspapers (even on the front page of *The New
York Times,* which seldom plays up murder) of the slaying of
Sharon Tate, a leading Hollywood actress who appeared in

the movie *Valley of the Dolls*. She was the wife of the young Polish director, Roman Polanski, whose American triumph was *Rosemary's Baby*. At the time of the murder he was in London.

Miss Tate, eight and a half months pregnant, was slain along with four others at her $200,000 rented mansion on a hillside at the end of Cielo Drive, set above Benedict Canyon, in Bel Air, California. The house was hidden in the woods behind a locked wrought-iron gate.

At 8:30 on Saturday morning, August 9, Mrs. Winifred Chapman arrived for the daily housecleaning at the Tate estate. She never reached the inside of the spreading red and beige house. She passed through the gate, crossed the driveway and parking area and came upon two bodies and blood spattered all over the grass. She stumbled in panic to a neighbor's house and awakened a fifteen-year-old boy who called the police.

Police found slumped behind the wheel of a white Rambler parked in the driveway the body of an eighteen-year-old youth, Steven Parent, who had been shot five times. On the lawn in front of the house sprawled the body of Wociech (Voityck) Frykowski, thirty-seven, fully clothed in "mod" attire. He was a childhood friend of Polanski's and his family had helped finance some of the director's first films in Poland. Frykowski followed Polanski to America, hoping to find a niche for himself in the movie industry. About twenty yards from his body, beneath a fir tree, curled the body of Abigail Folger, twenty-six, coffee heiress, who had been living with Frykowski in a house one canyon away. She was clad in a blood-drenched nightgown.

In the living room of the house police found the bodies of Miss Tate, twenty-six, and male hair stylist, Jay Sebring, thirty-five, once her fiancé. She was wearing a see-through nightgown and maternity bra. He was fully clothed. They lay a few feet apart. Around each was twisted a nylon rope that had been looped over a rafter. Both bodies bore savage stab wounds. Frykowski and Sebring had also been shot. The word "Pig" was written in blood on the front door.

In a guesthouse facing the driveway, police found nineteen-year-old William Garretson, hired a few months earlier as the caretaker. He said Parent had left his cottage about 12:15 A.M., after which Garretson turned on his stereo, wrote letters, and heard nothing out of the ordinary. At first police placed him under arrest but he was released after two days.

The following night in the Los Feliz district of midtown Los Angeles, Leno LaBianca, forty-four, owner of four large supermarkets, and his wife, Rosemary, thirty-eight, were found slain in their home. He lay on the living room floor in his pajamas, drenched with blood from stab wounds, a long meat fork protruding from his stomach and the word "War" carved on his chest. A pillowcase covered his head. His wife's body, clad in a sheer nightdress, lay in the master bedroom with so many knife wounds in her back that police said it looked like marks from a whipping. Written in blood on the refrigerator in the kitchen were the words, "Death to Pigs." The police suspected the same killers might have committed these murders.

At first police thought the slayers might be members of the Mafia, since Frykowski was allegedly involved in drug traffic. Four months later, when police finally made an arrest, the nation was almost as shocked by the identity of the suspected killers as it had been by the bloody crimes.

Three were twenty-one years and under; one was nineteen. They were members of a hippie group which called itself the "family," led by Charles Miller Manson, thirty-four, hailed at times as "Jesus," and at other times as "Satan." He supposedly was not present during the murders but had ordered his "slaves" to commit them.

The case broke when twenty-one-year-old Susan Atkins, in jail charged with having helped Robert Beausoleil kill Gary Hinman, a musician, at his home in July, 1969, confessed to a cellmate her part in the Tate murders. She also implicated two men and three young women in the Tate and LaBianca murders. The men were Manson and Charles Watson, twenty-four, known as "Tex." The young women were Leslie Van Houghton, nineteen, Patricia Krenwinkel, twenty-one, and Linda Kasabian, twenty.

While one reason for the shock to the nation was the fact that those charged with the murder were so youthful, a second and, perhaps, more significant reason was the further fact that the accused slayers did not know their victims. The killings seemed senseless. The victims were innocent people who had done their slayers no wrong.

It developed that in the Tate slaying there was a subtly insane motive. Manson, who desperately wanted a record made of a song he had composed, held a grudge against the young man who had rented the house before the Polanskis— Terrence Melcher, son of Doris Day. Melcher had supposedly backed out of an agreement to help Manson sell a record. In desire for revenge, one year later Manson was supposed to have ordered his "slaves" to slaughter everyone living in the house, no matter who they were.

If so, this was psychotic thinking on his part—use of the house as a symbol of the person who had rejected him. But calling Manson "psychotic" means little, for the word too often serves as a dead-end diagnosis, blocking any attempt to understand the amount of anger, and its causes, that whirls in the mind of the severely emotionally disturbed person— anger so intense it drives him to the insane behavior.

There appears much evidence Manson had to be the angriest of children. Murder, as Freud said, begins in the nursery. All later targets are, in the unconscious part of the mind, one's mother or father, or whoever brought up the murderer. Those slain are symbols of the first wicked giants in a child's life.

It is difficult to conceive of a childhood more traumatic than Manson's. If ever a boy must have felt unwanted and rejected, it was he. (This is not to condone his savagery but to understand it.) He was illegitimate, his father unknown, born in Cincinnati to a sixteen-year-old prostitute who must have hated him from the moment she knew she was pregnant. A year after he was born, she was sent to jail for eight years, convicted with her brother of beating up and robbing the men she hustled in riverfront bars.

When his mother went off to jail, Manson as a baby was sent to his maternal grandmother in McMechan, West Virginia, who lived with his aunt and uncle (and we can only guess how happy they were to receive an illegitimate baby to bring up). According to one report, they "tolerated him as long as he didn't cry for food, wet the bed or seek any affection from them." The aunt was a harsh woman who punished him severely when he disobeyed.

Manson grew up in McMechan until he was thirteen, when his uncle fell ill. He was sent to rejoin his mother, now out of jail, in Indianapolis. Again she gave evidence of not wanting him around. She was living in cheap hotels with a succession of men and she tried to get her son placed in foster homes. Finally she sent him to the Gibault School in Terre Haute, a boarding school run by Roman Catholic priests. She could not keep up the payments and the boy was returned to her. He did not stay long, he later told juvenile officials, because his mother was frequently drunk, lived with many men, and "I didn't want to stay where Mother lived in sin."

At the age of fourteen, he rented his own room and tried to support himself by delivering messages for Western Union and engaging in petty thefts, starting a life of crime that, for the next eighteen years, was to take him in and out of penitentiaries. His mother soon left Indianapolis after being arrested for adultery.

About this time, young Manson, a slight, short youth with a handsome, somewhat cherubic face, came to the attention of the Reverend George Powers, a local priest, who described him as looking like "an innocent altar boy" and remarked that Manson was "ashamed of his mother." Father Powers arranged for him to be sent to Boys Town near Omaha, Nebraska. The Indianapolis newspaper ran his picture and a story headlined "Boy Leaves 'Sinful Home' for New Life in Boys Town."

"He won everybody over," the priest recalled. "He had an ability beyond his years to present himself. He was a beautiful kid for his age." (As Susan Atkins and others were later to describe him as "beautiful.")

Manson arrived in Boys Town in March, 1949. He tolerated it for four days. He ran away, stealing a motor scooter, then a car. He was arrested while robbing a grocery store (robbing, just as his mother robbed the men she hustled) in Peoria, Illinois, and sent back to Indianapolis and his first correctional institution—the Indiana Boys School in Plainfield.

He was then shuffled from reform school to reform school, and later, from jail to jail and prison to prison, so that when last released from a federal penitentiary in March, 1967, he had spent more than twenty of his thirty-three years in institutions. He was arrested thirty-seven times for such crimes as stealing cars, theft, forgery, violation of probation. Once, on parole from the federal reformatory in Chillicothe, Ohio, at the age of twenty-one, he went back to McMechan to live with his grandmother and aunt and married a waitress who worked in a local hospital. They later had a son, but by the time the baby was born, Manson was in jail in California for transporting stolen vehicles.

In 1960 he was arrested for violating the White Slave Traffic Act in Laredo, Texas. The father of a Michigan girl who went to Los Angeles to study to be an airline stewardess, accused Manson of being "a sex maniac" when his daughter nearly died in a hospital operating room, the father claimed, as a result of sexual indiscretions involving Manson. Another young woman, friend of the Michigan girl, claimed Manson had drugged her, then forced her to have sexual relations with him.

While at McNeil Island penitentiary in the State of Washington, Manson became interested in rock music, philosophy, and Scientology, a pseudo-religious cult then popular on the West Coast. After he was released from prison, on March 21, 1967, he headed for the Haight-Ashbury district of San Francisco where the hippie movement was in full bloom. He started to gather around him his "family," composed chiefly of girls who seemed mesmerized by him. A friend attributed Manson's so-called magical power to his ability to have day-long sex orgies with one girl after another.

One of the girls in the "family," a nineteen-year-old college dropout who would identify herself only as Diane, told reporters why she thought girls were willing to be Manson's "slaves." She said, "With him, we were all important, we were all somebody. . . . Nobody ever bothered anybody out there at the ranch, they just asked me my name and I told them it was Diane. . . . It was beautiful out there. . . . We

94

got up when we wanted, we slept when we wanted and for the first time in my life there weren't any rules, except Charlie wouldn't let us kill any animals and we didn't eat meat. . . . It was like a big family. They were all my brothers and sisters. There wasn't any dissension, not even about sex.

"We would listen to Charlie preach about how we were the only ones who loved each other, and we were going to be the only ones left and we would build this new culture. . . . It's like nobody else counted but us. He explained how there wasn't any right and wrong, just what we felt was right for us. . . . Charlie had told us that when someone came in with a stolen car or a credit card or something, that they weren't stealing. He said we were just taking what we needed from people who didn't need it. He said we had a right to take it because we were going to be the only ones who mattered."

While on the surface Manson appeared kind, understanding, "beautiful," his anger often exploded, giving a clue to the intense fury that simmered underneath the smiling mask. When a neighbor at the Spahn ranch, an abandoned movie lot and riding stable thirty miles from Los Angeles in Chatsworth where the "family" lived, complained about the noise of motorcycle racing late at night by members of the "family," Manson told him, "Shut up, you son of a bitch, or I'll burn your goddamn house down." Some friends called him "Hymie" behind his back, meaning Hitler.

His anger was usually, but not always, directed at those he considered successful, for he hated the establishment, the affluent. But it could also be directed against his peers. One girl said she was hitchhiking to San Francisco with him with two big packs and "he wanted me to carry both of them." She said, "I refused. I said I'd share, but I wouldn't carry both. He got more and more angry and finally said I had to carry both bags and walk ten steps behind him. When I wouldn't do that, he took my guitar from me and smashed it into little pieces against a post."

Once he told a girl, "Follow my orders or meet a horrible death."

Here we see part of the emotional sickness in Manson as he acted like a furious baby who insists his every wish be fulfilled, who can brook no frustration, take no responsibility.

He would allow no one to harm a snake, and snakes were plentiful in the desert ranch (the phallic significance of "snake" is evident). He collected guns and ammunition and carried and "fondled," according to a *Life* magazine report, a Bowie knife.

"He really loved knives," said a friend. "He used to say, 'Man, everybody in this world is afraid of getting cut.' "

Manson threatened a young man who once followed Linda Kasabian to the ranch to protest her being there, "Maybe I should kill you just to show you there's no such thing as dying."

On the other hand, he said to a friend, "If you don't have someone to love you, you don't have anything. That's all there is, man."

This friend, Juan Flynn, told a reporter for *The New York Times,* in recalling a conversation with Manson, that the latter said, "Juan, when they catch me, it's going to be like feeding me to the lions. They're going to put me far away because I have no family, no one that will help me. When I was in jail, I noticed the bulls [guards] in there used to keep track of everything—the letters you got, the visitors who remembered you in there. I knew they could do anything to me, because I had nobody."

Having nobody is damaging emotionally to a child. But there are children who grow up having nobody and who do not turn into vicious murderers. Something else accounted for the rage in Manson's life that made it impossible for him to control his murderous wrath—the fact that he had a mother, an angry child herself, who was a prostitute and who, with her brother, beat up her "johns" and robbed them. In the first year of his life, Manson lived in the aura of sexual violence; it was his birthright. Twelve years after he left his mother, when he returned to live with her, he saw her take on one man after another, then get arrested for adultery. He did not need to have fantasies about his mother as a "whore" and a "bad woman," as Freud said most sons do at one time or another. Manson's mother *was* a whore and a "bad" woman. She instilled in him no moral standards whatsoever, and the prisons in which he spent most of his later life must have been equally devastating to him, morally speaking. Manson made his girls have sex with anyone he chose, just as his mother had sex with anyone she chose.

One friend of Manson's told a reporter that Manson began to talk of a "revolution" about eight months before the Tate killing. "He said he was building a bunch of dune buggies," recalled the friend. "He said he was going to mount machine guns on them. He said he'd take his army of dune buggies and kill every white mother—every white pig—between here and the desert."

Manson's hatred of the "white mother," the "white pigs," was burning hatred of his own mother, the "pig" in his life. He wanted to kill, as he felt she had killed him, she and all the men who had taken her away from him when he needed her as a baby and as a growing boy. Susan Atkins said they wanted "to kill, and shock the establishment," and the establishment was authority, or the parents of earlier days.

All those charged with taking part in the murders had to feel this way about their parents. Even the "All American" youth, Charles "Tex" Watson, the youngest of three children born to Mr. and Mrs. C. D. Watson, operators of a service station and general store in Copeville (population 150), twenty-five miles northeast of Dallas, Texas. The six-feet, two-inch "Tex" was a high school star in athletics and studies. After three years at North Texas State University, he became restless, dropped out and moved to California, where he got involved with drugs. He was the one, according to Susan's story which she later repudiated, supposedly after talking to Manson, who cut the telephone wires at the Tate house, stole into the home and opened the front door for the others, then stabbed Miss Tate to death as she pleaded with him to let her live so she could have her baby.

Perhaps it was the charged participation of so many young women in the murders that was most shocking. They had been thrown out of their homes or run away, came from broken homes or homes where one or both parents were alcoholic. Patricia Krenwinkel's father had left wife and daughter when the latter was in her early teens. Linda Kasabian, whose parents were divorced, was twice married at twenty, had one baby, and was five months pregnant. Max Lerner wrote of the "slaves," in his column, "The Rootless," in the New York *Post,* that "the sickening excuse that they were hypnotized by his [Manson's] 'orders to kill' is only confirmation of their own emptiness."

For emptiness, substitute anger, desire for sadistic revenge, and schizophrenia. One has to be slightly schizophrenic to commit murder or take part in a murder plot on the "order" of someone else. This is but one step removed from the schizophrenic who hears a "voice" that instructs him to kill.

The members of Manson's cult, acting as "slaves," did their leader's bidding just as they once did the bidding of their mother and father. They felt the world owed them a living, and anyone who would not take care of them deserved to die. The "family" made friends with musical celebrities, including Gary Hinman, the musician who let them stay in his home at Malibu for a while, then asked them to leave. He was found murdered in July, 1969, and Susan was accused of taking part in the killing. When someone refused to continue to give them food and shelter, the "family," under Manson's orders, apparently murdered him.

It is suspected by the police that the group took part in killing at least twenty victims. They looted, blackmailed, committed arson, stole cars, and forged credit cards, while traveling around Southern California in a bus used as headquarters. Police, in planes and dune buggies, finally flushed them out of a mountain hideout in Death Valley. When arrested, the girls were either nude or wore only bikini bottoms and carried sheathed knives. They were all undernourished. Several had given birth to babies that members of the "family" delivered.

These young people acted like little animals, licking the hand of whoever would feed them, wandering from one eating place to the next. They had no roots, no adherence to anyone. The love they felt they never got from parents, they sought from peers. They supported each other emotionally; they stole together, they slept together, they had sex together. They were children trying to act as parents but angry children acting as angry parents. The sadism was clear. They possessed a sadistic quality that enabled them to kill animalistically, like the matador kills the bull because it is a symbol of power and strength for him to do so. These angry young people, as they faced Sharon Tate, who had beauty, success, and wealth, thought of her dead with sadistic pleasure.

The girls were like a band of prostitutes, with Manson as the pimp who controlled his "stable" (one wonders if his mother had a pimp, or what her brother's role was). His girls stole for him, begged for him, took sex as lightly as they did

99

other people's possessions. The boys in the "family" shared the girls although, as one said, "Charlie always had first crack at the new girl."

They formed the "bad" family, in caricature of their parents. It was a schizophrenic family, the outgrowth of early emotional deprivation. They were, in a sense, reenacting the primal scene. To a child's irrational mind, the sex act resembles a man trying to murder a woman (or a woman killing a man, depending on the sexual position). One wonders how many times as a baby in his crib Manson saw his mother indulging in sex. He would not have understood what was going on in the bed but he would have been frightened and perhaps also fascinated.

In an interview on February 15, 1970, with Joe Hyams, the first journalist allowed to interview Manson, for a special story in the *National Enquirer,* Manson said his first crime was being born without a father. Hyams found Manson to be "a combination of James Dean and the Maharishi," and reported that he talked in a quiet voice, not hypnotic, but persuasive, as he constantly fingered his beard.

Manson told Hyams, "We are all programmed by our parents or the people who brought us up. People tell a child he's bad and he'll be bad. They tell him not to do something and that's the thing he'll do."

He also said, "All my life all I've ever known is rough people, people who didn't want any part of me for the most part." This was certainly true of his mother and no doubt of his grandmother, aunt, and uncle.

Of his years in jail: "So I learned all there is to learn from reform schools. You spend twenty years in jail with rough people who know what's going on in the world and you learn. . . . The thing that's good about prison is they kill your ego. I'm not just me. I'm everyone."

He spoke proudly of acquiring so many girls to take care of him, telling how they would get up early in the morning and "grub for food and prepare breakfast and they'd wake me. They know I like a hot bath so they'd have the water heated for me and then they'd bathe me."

This is what struck him as most important, as it would an emotionally deprived person whose own mother never took the time to care for him.

This was not *folie a deux* (crazy behavior condoned by two people who share the same mad fantasies) but *folie a quinze* or *vingt*. We do not think of teen-agers living in a hippie commune as bent on murder, and most are not, for they stress "peace" and "love," and try to hide or deny their angry feelings. But this was a special "family" which attracted those as angry as youth can get, a family dedicated to free-floating sex and murder.

Those charged with killing or taking part in the murder of Sharon Tate are extreme cases, as I have said. But the extreme, in its distortion, illuminates the average. The extreme displays in detail and exaggerated form that which lies in all of us. All of us as children, and occasionally as adults, *feel* like committing murder when someone hurts or frustrates us. But we do not act on the wish. We are able to control our impulse to kill.

The terrifying emotional illness of Susan Atkins can clearly be seen in her story of her childhood and her part in the murders, in the book *The Killing of Sharon Tate* by Lawrence Schiller and two other journalists who worked with him as a team but who wanted to be kept anonymous.

Without labeling Susan as schizophrenic, Schiller describes schizophrenic qualities in her. He tells how sometimes, when talking to him, she broke into her own words with sudden humming, or mispronounced a long word, or used it out of context, as a schizophrenic will. Sometimes, he said, uttering a nervous laugh she would lick her lips. He commented, "Does she really mean what she is saying? Can she distinguish fantasy from fact?"

Susan's own words paint a tragic portrait of her early life with an alcoholic father who called her a "slut" (when a father accuses his daughter of this, the girl, out of anger, may become one) and beat his wife, just as Susan's older brother would beat her. Here again we see a child brought up with violence in the house so that it becomes almost a way of life.

Susan said of Manson, "I love him. I'll always love him. I am him and he is me." This is how a baby feels about its mother, that he and she are one. The schizophrenic in fantasy lives in the early days of infancy, unable to move out of his precarious emotional attachment to his mother. Susan both hated and yearned for her mother. When Susan was almost fifteen, her mother died of cancer. Susan said she could not cry at the funeral, that she could not wait for her mother to die: "I wanted to get rid of her. She was just in my way." And yet when her grandmother came to live with them, Susan said she did not like her "because she was taking my mother's place and I knew nobody could take my mother's place." Here we see the intense love-hate confusion of the schizophrenic.

In Susan's story, a wished-for incestuous relationship with her father becomes evident. She believes her father wanted to have an affair with her after her mother died because he treated her basically the way he treated her mother. This could be in large part her wish, fulfilling her fantasies about her father. She even says this: "I actually did want to have an affair with him. Yes. He was my father and I loved him." Then she says all little girls want to have affairs with their fathers and all fathers want to have affairs with their little girls. This is not true, for although there may be such a wish,

102

it is usually repressed, appearing only in dreams—if then.

Another evidence of schizophrenia appears when, after starting to go out with men, frequenting bars, getting drunk, and letting men take her to motel rooms and "do what they wanted to do with me" (at eighteen, Susan was doing sexually what Manson's mother did at sixteen), she says she would return home and deny such things ever happened to her because she was "a nice girl."

When Manson first had sexual relations with her (he did so only four times in the two years they were together, according to her), he asked if she had ever made love with her father. She said no. He then asked if she had ever thought about it. She became embarrassed, she confessed. While Manson and she were engaged in the act of sex, he told her to imagine she was making love with her father. She called it the most beautiful experience she'd ever had. Here we see the fantasied incestuous intimacy in which the "family" lived. When Susan decided to join Manson and four girls and travel in a bus he provided, she was willing to share him sexually with the other girls. She admitted she was afraid of him although he fascinated her (the way she felt about her father). One moment Manson would tell her he loved her completely, the next, that she was not afraid enough of him and he did not know what it would take to put that fear into her.

Susan said she left the establishment the minute she stepped on Manson's bus. She called the establishment "the beast." This is the "pig," the mother and father of childhood, the word Susan said she wrote in blood on Sharon Tate's front door, ordered to do so by Charles Watson, after, she said, he had killed Sharon Tate and the others.

Susan described how she kept a "headlock" hold on Miss Tate who pleaded, "All I want to do is to have my baby." In Susan's words: "I knew I had to say something to her before

103

she got hysterical. And while I was talking to her, I knew everything I was saying—I was saying to myself. I wasn't talking to her, but myself.

" 'Woman, I have no mercy for you,' I told her, and that was myself talking only to me."

Here is similarity between Susan's attitude toward her own mother and Miss Tate. She had no mercy for either. As she said, she was glad when her mother died.

Susan claimed that Watson stabbed Sharon Tate in the heart again and again, then, as they all ran out of the house, ordered her to go back and write something on the door. She took the towel with which she had tied Frykowski's hands and went over to Sharon Tate. In her words, "And I flashed. Wow, there's a living being in there. . . . I wanted to, but I couldn't bring myself to cut her open and take the baby. I knew it was living. I knew it wouldn't live. . . . I could hear the blood inside her body gurgling. It wasn't a very pretty sound. I know now that's called the death rattle." She dipped the towel in Miss Tate's blood and then wrote "PIG" on the door.

What Susan's fantasies were when her mother was pregnant with her younger brother, only Susan knows. But she may have been wildly jealous and wished to destroy the fetus inside her mother. Such vicious acting-out as she displayed as a participant in the killings has to contain a wish from childhood in it. Also, when one childhood wish is intense, such as Susan's desire to sleep with her father, many childhood emotions are apt to be intensified, such as jealousy.

An interesting facet is the fact that Susan Atkins was the one to turn in Manson and the rest as she told her story to a cellmate in the Los Angeles County jail for women. Why did she confess?

One youth remembered her as Manson's most devoted

follower. She constantly praised Manson to others. This young man recalled, "Susie said the only way to join the Family was to agree to give up your life for all members of the group. She once handed me an ax and put her head down. She said, 'Go ahead and kill me.' That kind of shook me up."

Manson told her she did not fear him the way the others did. Perhaps that was one reason she could betray him.

We might guess, from what we know of her background, that one of Susan's motives in telling on Manson was to get revenge on the man, she believed, had turned her into a slut and prostitute, ordering her to sleep with any young man who might wander into the commune. The revenge was really on her father, the one who had called her a slut and a prostitute.

She and Manson acted out their own *folie a deux,* as they mutually took part in the incestuous fantasy that, when they had sex, he was her father (and how much guilt that must have aroused, for our strongest taboo is incest). As Manson had sex with her, and ordered her to sleep with other men, he could then in fantasy think of her as his mother, the prostitute. Manson undoubtedly was getting revenge on the woman he felt had deserted him in infancy for many men.

Another of Susan's motives for confessing might be the wish to stop herself from taking part in future murders. She said she felt "killed" when she returned from the Tate slaughters and this was her guilt, the feeling she should be dead for what she had done. Since she was the one least afraid of Manson, it was logical she be the one strong enough to put a stop to the wanton slaughters.

From what we know of the early lives of Manson and his "slaves," we can assume they were the angriest of children. Their parents either never helped them learn the control needed to handle their natural hostile impulses, or else made them "overcontrol" themselves so that one day their hostility was bound to erupt. Manson's aunt and uncle, with whom he lived between the ages of one and thirteen, forced him to repress all manifestations of anger and be a "good" boy.

Studies by leading psychoanalysts reveal that angry children also possess parents who unconsciously condone the child's anger. Such parents permit the child to carry out assaultive acts of which the parents unconsciously approve. They do not stop the child's temper tantrums. They make no effort to understand the child's rage, or their own. They do not care enough about themselves or the child to be able to help him mature psychically.

As he himself pointed out, nobody ever cared about Charles Manson. According to one of the girls, he had "the look that he needs to be mothered." Again and again, in the study of murderers, one fact stands out: the wish on the part of the mother that she had never borne the child.

An adult hates excessively only if he has been hated excessively as a child by his mother or father or both. One important fact in the Oedipus myth is often overlooked. In killing his father and bringing about the suicide of his mother, Oedipus was getting even with his parents because *they* had ordered *him* murdered as a baby (a kindly shepherd saved his life). It seems to be the unwanted child who has the most trouble controlling his murderous impulses.

Every mother has some feeling of ambivalence about her child. Seldom is an emotion pure. But it is the degree to which a mother's hatred outweighs her love that, in large part, will determine the amount of anger in the child. A child can tell, in day-to-day living, if his mother hates him more than she loves him.

The greatest hatred a mother can show a child is to abandon him. The mother who deserts a child, as Manson's mother deserted him, by going to jail for eight years (a child cannot understand *why* his mother leaves, he only knows she has vanished) is laying the grounds for murder. It does not always come out as a murder of others, for the child as an adult may commit suicide, or become psychotic (psychic murder). If the child is lucky enough to have a strong father and a loving stepmother, as Leonardo da Vinci did, he may turn his grief to genius (Leonardo's mother was forced to abandon him to his father, a wealthy man who did not want to marry the servant he had made pregnant but who wanted to bring up his son).

The fury with which a child may react when his mother walks out on him was shown by a six-year-old boy, brought to me by his father, a wealthy financier with a passion for hunting. When he called me about his son, he said, in a voice choked with emotion, "Tommy is uncontrollable in school. He lives alone with me and I can't control him either. Please try to help us."

He told me that Tommy's mother had left home when he was four to marry another man. (The earlier psychic damage is done to a child, the more devastating it is. In the first years of life, a child possesses little ability to reason and his fantasies run wild. He is full of primitive impulses he cannot control. He has no way of coping with those who hurt him. If his anger runs deep, he may vow revenge later in life when he has become a stalking giant himself.)

As Tommy walked in for his first session, I saw an alert-looking little boy, sturdily built, with keen brown eyes and a rather sensitive face.

Two strides in, and Tommy's eyes lit on Rusty, my small red cocker spaniel who sometimes keeps children company during their sessions. Rusty is very attracted to little patients and greets them with his tail wagging. Most children pat him lovingly, sensing his friendliness, and he licks their hands and

107

faces if they pick him up. A few are afraid and back away. Then, as though sensing their fear, Rusty quietly patters to a corner of the room and lies down, sometimes to doze.

Seeing Tommy, Rusty eagerly moved towards him, anticipating a loving pat. Instead, Tommy's foot shot out in a sudden kick at Rusty's head. It was such a fierce, well-aimed kick that it knocked the little dog unconscious. He rolled to the floor, his head lolling against it.

At this moment I was truly shocked. I, who had believed myself unshockable, who had talked calmly to murderers in Bellevue Hospital's prison ward, who had heard many stories of man's inhumanity to man, was aghast at the open cruelty of this little boy.

I rushed over to Rusty, picked him up gently. Luckily he was soon groping his way back to consciousness and licking my hand. Putting him down, I said to Tommy, my voice barely able to hold back my fury, "Please sit in this chair," indicating the one across from my desk.

Then, seating myself as calmly as I could, I asked, "Why did you do that to my little dog? That was the cruelest act I have ever seen."

"If I did what I do to other animals, it would hurt your dog more." His voice was casual, as though he had treated Rusty with great gallantry.

"What do you do to other animals?" I asked, awaiting new cruelty.

"I killed a cat yesterday by torturing it." The voice was still casual.

"How?" I was determined to find out all the facts, to learn what drove this little boy, who looked so innocent, to such sadism.

"I tortured it to death by sticking a knife into its neck very slowly, over and over, each time deeper, until it was dead," he said. Then he added, "And I kill flies by pulling off their legs. I like to kill."

"Why?" I asked.

Tommy shrugged his slight shoulders. His brown eyes looked coolly into mine, his face impassive. He said, "My father teaches me to kill."

"What do you mean?" I was puzzled

"He takes me hunting with him all the time and I see him kill deer. Sometimes we go fishing and I see him slice live fish apart with his knife. But he likes hunting better. He has lots of guns at home hanging on the wall. He says he always shoots to kill."

It is not the guns hanging on the wall, I thought, but the child's rage that makes him want to use those guns. Another child, one not so angry, would ignore the guns.

"But your father kills animals, not people," I pointed out to Tommy.

"People, too," Tommy said and the first sign of emotion came into his voice.

"What do you mean?" I had visions of his father being a Jack the Ripper.

In a voice that now faltered because it held so much feeling, Tommy said, "I heard my father tell my mother on the telephone, 'I'm going to kill you if you ever come into this house again.' "

How literally children take every word uttered, I thought. Parents *must* remember everything they say a child will assume to be true. A child dwells in a world of black and white, right and wrong, good and bad.

"When did your father threaten to kill your mother?" I asked.

"Just after she walked out on us. About two years ago."

"Why do you think she left, Tommy?"

109

"She fell in love with my father's best friend. She wanted a divorce. At first my father said he would rather see her dead than let her leave us. But then one night he got real mad and threw her out and said if she ever came back he'd kill her with one of the guns on the wall. And he tells her the same thing every time she calls to speak to me."

"Do you see your mother?"

"The judge makes my father let me visit her one Sunday every month. But I don't like to go. I don't like George. That's her new husband."

It is far easier to hate a stepfather than a real parent, I thought. I asked, "Why don't you like him?"

"He tries to be nice to me but I know he hates me."

"Maybe it's you that hates him."

"I don't hate anybody," he said, as though he believed this.

"Then why do you torture and kill innocent animals?"

He was silent.

"Nobody tortures and kills animals unless he also feels this way about people," I said. "Generally the people closest to him."

Still silence.

I ventured a suggestion. "Do you hate your mother for leaving you?"

Silence.

He would talk no more that session. But he came back the following week and regularly thereafter three times a week. One day he started to talk, in a faltering voice, about his mother, and tears slipped down his cheeks which he quickly brushed away. The next session, as he was telling of a visit to her home, he burst forth with, "I hate her for leaving me! If she cared about me, she never would have gone!"

His mother's desertion meant she did not love him, that she wished him dead. He was saying to me: "My mother

110

abandoned me. I could have died, for all she cared." To him this was torture. He was being pulled apart as he had pulled apart the fly, he was being knifed as he had knifed the cat, he was being kicked in the head as he had kicked Rusty.

"My mother has killed me by leaving me. I am too young to be left alone. I am so angry I want to kill her, just like my father wants to kill her. I even have Dad's permission to kill her," little Tommy was saying.

He could not kill his mother but he could vent his murderous wrath on little insects and animals who could not fight back.

Tommy remained with me for two years and, as he gradually brought himself to speak frankly about his anger at his mother, and his father, too—whom he blamed for the loss of his mother, for being unable to hold her at home—Tommy gave up brutality to animals. He was no longer a problem at school, behaving normally in class.

During this period I had several talks with his father and pointed out how important it was that he not take Tommy hunting. I advised him, instead, to take his son to baseball games or other sports events where the slaughter of an animal was not the goal.

As he became aware of his anger at his mother, Tommy was able to embrace her warmly and also to talk to her and tell her how he felt. I helped him understand that because his mother could no longer get along with his father did not mean she hated her son. Children believe the whole world revolves around them. It is difficult for them to understand they are not always the sole object in their mother's life, that her relationship to her husband may be even more important to her at the moment. Her escape from a husband she hates and who hates her may determine a wife's sanity. It may even involve her safety, for she may be fleeing for her very life, as I thought,

111

at times, Tommy's mother might have been, should her husband lose control of himself and grab one of his guns from the wall.

Unlike Manson, unlike Tommy, are those who cannot bear the thought of violence even though they may be suffering from repressed murderous wishes. One youth who came to see me was just the reverse of Tommy on the surface. Ronald was a sixteen-year-old boy who winced at the thought of firing a gun.

He was sent by his parents because he was depressed and would not go to school. A tall youth, emaciated looking, he trudged slowly into my office as though on his way to the electric chair. He sat down reluctantly. At first there was a faraway look in his eyes. Then he turned to me with a deeply hostile stare, the large blue eyes holding an almost demonic glare. And then, unexpectedly, the glare swiftly turned into a smile, but it was the smile of a Cheshire cat, a smile that was mechanical and false.

Ronald was dressed neatly and had a crew cut, unusual in this day and age of the hippie troubadour tumbling locks.

"I'm here because my parents think there's something wrong with me," he stated curtly. "But I don't think there's anything wrong. Just because I don't want to go into the service and fight a war in which I don't believe, my friends at school, and my father, call me a coward. I will *not* use a gun —against a man or an animal."

He added, "My father also thinks I'm a sissy because when he takes me hunting, I will not kill a deer. Once I tried to aim at the animal but the gun slipped out of my hand, fell on my foot, and broke a bone in my toe. The next time he took me hunting, I threw the gun on the ground and stamped on it."

I wondered why this father insisted on taking along on a

112

hunting trip a son who so obviously did not want to kill. Probably "to make a man of him," I thought ironically, as though slaying a deer makes a man of anyone, even though it may momentarily give a sense of power to a man who does not feel a man within himself.

Beneath Ronald's mechanical smile I sensed a depressed, hostile, and apprehensive youth, facing a stint in the armed services which he feared, as he told me, "My friends have deserted me. They all want to go into the Army and kill, they say."

"Perhaps they protest too much, covering up their fear of killing and being killed by pretending to be brave," I said. "You at least are honest about the way you feel."

Tears slid into his eyes. "Thank you for saying that," he said. "You seem to understand how I feel."

I understood something else, too—that he wanted to cry because he did not want to die so early in life.

"I understand how you feel about killing," I assured him. "Killing another human being who has done you no wrong is not an act of courage, but the act of a sick, destructive human being. If your bragging friends, who probably want to shock you, really mean what they say—that they *want* to kill— then there is something wrong with them." (Incidentally, I am the only woman psychiatrist to hold a presidential appointment as Consultant Medical Advisor to the Selective Service System.)

I asked Ronald, "How does your mother feel about your going into service?"

He hesitated, then said, "She doesn't want me to go. She's babied me all my life and she doesn't want me to have to face the hardships of army life."

I thought, The mother who babies her grown son will arouse in him many murderous wishes, for she overprotects and overcontrols him, which means he has to fight hard for his identity. This boy is afraid to lift a gun, in part, because he wishes to kill his mother, but this, of course, I cannot tell him. Perhaps, however, I can help him sense some of his rebellion against his mother.

"How do you feel about your mother's 'babying' you all your life?" I picked up his very words.

Again he hesitated. "I suppose it's her way of caring. But at times I get mad as hell because she thinks she knows better than I what I want to do."

"And 'mad as hell' at your father because he insists you kill an innocent deer?"

This time when he smiled it was a real smile, not a hypocritical gesture. "You really dig me," he said.

"It's human nature at the age of sixteen to resent overprotectiveness and to resent having to do something cruel which goes against your nature," I told him.

Ronald lost his depression and returned to high school in a matter of weeks. He came to see me for a year, at the end of which he was better prepared to deal with his fear of war. At the same time, he understood how his friends coped with their fear, overcompensating by denying it. Denial is one of our strongest psychic defenses against danger.

The fear of young men that they may die in battle is a real and acute emotion. What is stronger than the instinct to save one's life? Young girls face another kind of fear. They fear they will fall in love with a young man who will be sent off to war and die, abandoning them forever. Some girls also identify with the young men, suffer with them.

Thus, added to the natural anger that lies in all children —which has been part of childhood since Cain and Abel— today arises another cause of anger, connected with having to fight in a war about which many young people have no conviction. The reality of the Vietnam War as a cause of the rage and rebellion of youth cannot be dismissed. But it cannot be stressed as the *only* cause for their intense anger.

The anger in most young people is anger carried from the cradle and the early years of growing up. If, as in Manson's case, it explodes in wholesale murder, we cannot blame a war. The causes must be sought in what happens between a child and his mother during the first crucial years of the child's life. If he lives in terror, if terror to him is the familiar, he will have a need to inflict that terror on others in later years.

We are just starting to think in preventive terms, realizing that the earlier we can help our severely troubled children, not only will the children be happier, but society will eventually be spared countless murders, suicides, thefts—all types of criminal behavior.

If Charles Manson had received psychiatric help along the way, a number of persons—including Sharon Tate—would now be alive. You cannot send a youth to prison on and off for twenty years and expect him to come out anything but more vengeful than when he went in, if he is not helped to understand and come to grips with his original rebellion.

The more I work with today's children, the more I realize the troubled ones *have* to find a life that is satisfying. They need to know why they have been so angry. They need to feel their lives are worthwhile. They need to have depression lifted, rage eased. They need to express themselves, to believe in what America stands for—freedom of speech and thought and the right to the pursuit of happiness.

Our youth needs to know the difference between freedom and license. Freedom implies a certain control, a willingness to postpone the pleasure of the moment for future satisfaction. License is a giving-in to the whim of the moment, no matter

115

how destructive. The youth who is free is also the disciplined youth, the youth who can make choices that lead to constructive, not destructive behavior.

Freedom is the true power, not the slaughter of others, as the "slaves" and their leader, Manson, believed to be the road to power.

7.
DEATH
TO THE
BEDWETTER

AT THE SAME TIME AS THE ALLEGED SLAYERS OF SHARON TATE were caught in Los Angeles, a murder trial was in progress on the other side of the country. The one accused was not a youth but a forty-one-year-old man. He was on trial for the murder of a three-year-old child.

A stepfather, George Poplis, part-time waiter, was accused of beating little Roxanne Felumero to death with his fists and tossing her weighted body into the East River in Manhattan.

The charge was made in court that the mother had also beaten the little girl. The defense attorney, Manuel Steinberg, claimed that the mother, Marie, a narcotics addict, was equally to blame for the murder. He asserted that Poplis was "guilty of aiding and abetting the disposal of the body" but not of murder.

"George Poplis shouldn't be sitting in that chair," indicating the defendant. "Somebody else should be. Why wasn't Marie indicted for murder?"

He charged that Assistant District Attorney Gino Gallina got a confession out of Poplis by promising he would get "only three or four years" and on the assurance that the mother would not be indicted. But, said Steinberg, the uproar caused

117

by the case was so great "that the district attorney could no longer keep his bargain and that's why the defendant is sitting here today."

Gallina, in turn, charged that Poplis had hit the little girl "as hard as a man would hit another man."

He put on the stand as first witness Mrs. Rose Boccio, who for two years had been a foster mother to little Roxanne. Mrs. Boccio, wife of a cab driver, told the jury in a quavering voice that Roxanne was only ten months old when she came to live with her and she had learned to love the little girl. Mrs. Boccio remarked that the child would "throw up" whenever her mother visited.

At the end of two years, Roxanne, then three, was returned to her mother. When Mrs. Boccio visited Roxanne to take her to see the towering Christmas tree at Rockefeller Center on January 1, 1969, she noticed the child had a black eye and that her leg buckled under her. Later, when she bathed Roxanne at the Poplis home, she saw bruises on her back. The next day the Boccios took Roxanne to the New York Foundling Hospital to have her examined, and the day after that a hearing was held before Family Court. But Roxanne was allowed to stay with her mother.

Gallina, in describing how, after two years with the Boccios, the Family Court had decided to return Roxanne to her mother, said, "She was removed from the Boccio home, where she had been loved, and was thrust into a nightmare. It became more horrible in stages over a three-month period—rejection, isolation, savage beatings, terror, numbness, finally ending in death. All committed in the name of chastising her for wetting the bed, chastisement of a child who was well behaved."

He said further, "The week before her death, she was

beaten about the head so hard her face turned black, and her head became the size of two or three heads."

A twenty-one-year-old friend of the mother's, who was also a narcotics addict, described how she found little Roxanne mute and terrified, "her head swollen twice the normal size," huddled in a two-by-four-foot toilet in the Poplis apartment. Mrs. Donna Maksin testified she visited the Poplis apartment three times in ten days before Roxanne died and each time found the child in more pitiable condition.

On the first visit, she did not see Roxanne until she went to the bathroom about three hours after her arrival. She said, "I saw Roxanne huddled by the toilet, just sitting there. I put my hands out to her and said, 'Roxanne, come here baby.' She backed away like she was frightened. One eye was black, all black and blue. She was black and blue down her back from the top all the way down to her legs. Her head was twice the normal size, all out of proportion."

Mrs. Maksin said she stayed in the Poplis apartment several hours that day and "Roxanne never left the bathroom." Some days later she again visited Mrs. Poplis and found Roxanne much worse. She said, "The child's mouth was all busted open. The whole face was swollen. It was almost twice the size I last saw it."

She again saw Roxanne on the last day of the little girl's life. She said, "I saw Roxanne lying on the bed, covered up to her forehead. I only saw the top of her head but it was enormous." She said she thought the little girl was "scared to death."

In the account carried by the New York *Daily News,* Mrs. Carol Balet, formerly a case aide at the New York Foundling Hospital, testified she had recommended the return of Roxanne to her mother although she knew Mrs. Poplis had a history as a narcotics addict. Mrs. Balet said Roxanne was a "happy child" with her foster parents, the Boccios, who treated her like one of their own, but that Mrs. Poplis showed a continuing interest in getting her daughter back. Mrs. Balet said she knew the mother had suicidal tendencies, was a former addict, a former mental patient, and for two years had been a "floater" with no permanent address.

Poplis was found guilty by a jury of murder "under depraved circumstances" and sentenced to twenty years to life in prison. As a result of the case, the state legislature passed the Bill of Rights for Children which called for a separate part of Family Court to deal with child abuse cases.

In its way, this murder was as horrifying as the Tate slayings. There is something especially inhuman—subhuman we might say—when an adult kills a child, and his own child at that, the very one he is supposed to protect. The reason given for the beatings, as stated in the evidence, was that the little girl wet her bed at night. She was at an age when, according to Dr. Benjamin Spock, she should not be expected to do more than start to learn to control her excretory organs.

What is there about bedwetting that so infuriates a parent he often must punish—in this case, kill—a child who cannot establish control at once?

It has to do, on the surface, with the child's being "clean" rather than "dirty," "good" rather than "bad." The need to be "clean," to be "good," is one almost all parents drive home to a child as they attempt to civilize him. This they must do so he is able to live with others.

But when fear of "dirt" or of "wetting the bed" is excessive, when a demand is made on the child that he be "clean" beyond his ability to control himself, this is psychotic behavior. It may end, as it did with poor little Roxanne, in murder. She needed extra understanding for she was a troubled, insecure

120

little girl who vomited when she saw her own mother. Her fear would make it doubly hard for her to control the wetting of her bed, a symptom exhibited by many insecure children.

An underlying fear inherent in the word "dirty" is associated with sex, which, to a child, means masturbation. As I have said, parents who cannot accept that a certain amount of masturbation at the age of four or five or six is natural, that the child may not progress to the next phase of sexual development if he does not go through the masturbatory stage, may set the scene so that the child does not even dare masturbate.

Some parents, realizing how difficult it is for a child to first learn to control his bladder, may overindulge him, not requiring him to stop wetting the bed until he is seven or eight, which is far too late and creates emotional problems for the child. One mother brought in her eleven-year-old daughter because she had suddenly started to wet her bed again.

"Did she ever have a bedwetting problem?" I asked.

"When she was seven, she started to regress. She didn't become toilet-trained until she was five-and-a-half so I guess the regression was understandable," said this mother, who was being psychoanalyzed, had read Freud, and used the technical language quite freely. She added, "Tina is very tense and stimulated most of the time. She is precocious for her age, too. She had her first menstrual period a year ago."

When Tina came to me for treatment, I noticed she was quite a wiggler. She could not sit still one second but continually shifted around in the chair. At the private school she attended, the teacher reported she was incorrigible in that she would talk too much in class.

In spite of her incessant wiggling, Tina appeared to be a charming, pretty, dark-haired girl, full of energy and vitality but obviously not capable of channeling it wisely.

After her mother left my office, to wait in the reception

room, Tina said conspiratorially, "My mother bosses me all the time. I don't pay attention to her any more. All she ever says is 'don't, don't, don't, Tina.' "

"Why do you think you are wetting your bed, Tina?" I asked.

She squirmed around in the chair, her face flushing, then turned so her back was almost to me. I realized that, like her mother, she was embarrassed, as well she might be, at the thought of a girl of eleven wetting her bed.

"Don't be ashamed to talk about anything to me," I said. "Remember, I'm a doctor."

"But it has to do with a funny place," she said, only half-twisted away from me now.

"You can talk freely about any part of your body, Tina. You can talk about your head, your toes, your feet, and your abdomen. Or your belly-button. There is no part of your body of which you should be ashamed."

Then I asked, wondering if the bedwetting was connected with menstruation, "Did your mother tell you, before you got your period, that it was likely to happen?" Some mothers delay, and the shock to a little girl not prepared for menstruation may be a devastating one, although in this day and age most girls learn of it from classmates if a mother is negligent.

"She talked about it years ago," replied Tina. "She told me it was a way of getting ready to be a woman."

Tina was wriggling again and looking around the room, as many youngsters do when they first visit. She tried to divert my attention by picking up the glass pig from my desk and asking, "Where did you get this?"

"In Rome," I replied.

"And this?" She picked up the golden goat.

"In Paris."

122

"And that picture on the wall?"

"Montreal."

Believing the diversion had gone on long enough, I said, "Now may I ask you some questions, Tina?"

"Sure." She settled down in one spot on the chair for a moment, adopting a listening attitude as if, since I had responded to all her questions, she would answer mine.

"What has happened recently that might have caused you to wet your bed?"

She looked puzzled, as though trying to discover some plausible reason.

"Is it something your mother did?" I asked.

"No." She shook her head.

"Your father?"

"No."

Then she volunteered, "It's my teacher."

"What about your teacher?"

"I'm scared of her."

"Is she new to you this year?"

"Yes. She just came to the school."

"What day did school begin?"

"I think it was Monday, the second week in September."

"And when did you start wetting your bed?"

"Just after school began. My mother scolded me. She said I was too old for that sort of thing. Only children and babies wet their beds."

"How old is your teacher?"

"She's very old."

"Is she as old as I am?"

"I don't know how old you are. But you look very young. She's *really* old. And she has a very dark voice."

A wonderful description, I thought, of a voice that is frightening to a child.

Tina went on, "She wears glasses and looks half over them, and it feels as if she looks through you. She always yells and screams at us. The whole class is scared of her."

"Would you like to go to another school?"

"No. All my friends are there. We like the rest of the school. It's just this one teacher we hate. We want to get rid of her."

Tina was telling me she was no coward; she would not flee the school just because she was afraid of the teacher. In addition, she had allies in other pupils.

I said gently, "If you want to be strong enough to get rid of your teacher, you must first be strong enough within yourself to stop wetting your bed."

"I want to stop," she said wistfully. "That's why Mother brought me to see you."

When Tina's session ended, I called in her mother, asking Tina to wait in the reception room. I told her mother what Tina had said. I noticed how much the mother was an older version of her daughter—dynamic and restless, too, moving uneasily in the chair. It was easy to see how Tina unconsciously imitated her mother's movements.

All at once, the mother's posture became rigid as she sat up stiffly in the chair like a teacher at her desk, or a queen on her throne. She started to fire questions at me as though she were a district attorney and I a prisoner at the bench.

"What's the matter with Tina?"

"Have you found out why she wets her bed?"

"What has Tina told you about her father and me?"

Instead of answering directly, I asked, "Have you ever been a teacher?" curious to see if there were a direct connection between Tina's fear of her teacher and fear of her mother.

"Never!" The response was emphatic. "Although I once thought about it in college. But I got married right after graduating and Tina was born within a year." Then she again demanded, "What *is* wrong with Tina?"

This time I answered. "I think she and the other pupils in the class are having a difficult time with their new teacher. They are afraid of her. She seems too strict, too much of a disciplinarian."

"Tina *needs* to be disciplined," she insisted. "She runs wild at home. I go out of my wits trying to quiet her down. She *never* sits still."

Now I noticed the mother looked as if she might be pregnant. I asked, "Are you going to have a baby?"

She nodded. "I'm five months pregnant. My first child since Tina. We never thought we'd have another."

"That might be one reason Tina has started to wet her bed again," I said. "She has been the belle of your house for eleven years, and now suddenly a rival threatens to supersede her. Children may regress to a more dependent stage when they sense there will be a new baby in the home. Tina may be asking you not to forget she has needs, too. She wants you to love her as much as you will the new baby."

"Of course I will," she said hastily. "I know enough to do that. My own analyst has discussed that matter with me."

I did not want to interfere with her analyst. My job was Tina. I said, "Tina's fear of her teacher is deep but she doesn't want to leave the school or her classmates."

"What can I do about it?" She sounded earnest.

"You might speak to the principal, for one thing. Also, since you are in analysis, you must realize Tina's fear of the teacher is a transference of her fear of you. If she wasn't afraid of you, she would not fear the teacher so excessively that she has to wet her bed. Probably none of the other little girls has this problem."

The mother frowned. "I try to understand her."

"Are you very strict with her?" I asked. I added, "You certainly weren't when it came to toilet-training. She should probably have been trained earlier, for her own good."

Tears came into the mother's eyes. "Sometimes I can't help what I do. I know I treat her just like my mother treated me—strict about some things, not strict about others—and I hated my mother for what *she* did! I try to catch myself each time I scream at Tina or give her too many orders. I think I'm doing much better since I've been in analysis."

"I'm sure you are." I tried to reassure her. "Just keep showing Tina you love her and assure her you will love her no less when the new baby arrives. And do tell the principal that a number of girls in Tina's class are frightened of the new teacher with the 'dark voice.' "

This she did. The teacher was transferred to an older class of girls who, presumably, could accept her strictness more easily. Tina's bedwetting stopped, as her mother informed me via a telephone call. She did not get in touch with me again. It has been two years since the birth of the new baby so I presume Tina gave up her temporary regression.

There are realistic reasons why a boy or girl may suddenly start to wet the bed after they have been toilet-trained, or to regress in other ways, such as reverting to baby-talk or refusing to eat, or overeating. The birth of a brother or sister is one reason. This is a threatening period for every child who, up to that time, has been the baby of the household, its youthful tyrant.

Jealousy is a natural feeling among brothers and sisters and, unless it is intense and leads to violence, is not to be considered abnormal. A parent aware of his own feelings of jealousy can help a child accept his. Every child wants to be the "only" child. Every child needs to feel special in some way.

It is this feeling of being "special" that enables a child

126

to give up the egomaniacal feelings that are part of his psychic survival kit. A child should never be punished for showing feelings of jealousy. Instead, he should be given more attention, but attention that denotes affection and interest, not the attention sometimes given grudgingly by a parent to an angry child.

One sixteen-year-old girl brought to me for help was given all the attention in the world. She was an only child, the daughter of wealthy parents. The contrast between the daughter and the mother who brought her was almost laughable.

The mother was dressed in the highest of style. She wore an expensive tailored suit, a sable coat and hat, her fingernails were perfectly manicured and every blond hair in her elaborate headstyle was in place. The daughter looked (and smelled) as though she had not taken a bath in a month. She wore filthy blue jeans scissored around the edges, which had been cut to her knees, a torn sweater, sneakers, no stockings, and a threadbare coat. Her blond hair hung in limp masses on her shoulders.

Looking at the girl, it was hard to believe her parents had all the money in the world. They owned three homes in Europe—one in Ireland, one in France and one in Italy—as well as a mansion on Long Island, the scene of elaborate parties. They drove in Rolls Royces—nothing so plebian as a Continental or Cadillac for them. The father, a movie magnate, had also inherited vast oil fortunes from his father.

Along with wealth, the mother possessed an absolute fetish for perfection. She even had had all her teeth pulled and false ones put in so they would look perfect when she smiled.

About a year before, the father unexpectedly left home to divorce his wife, this "perfect" creature, and marry his secretary. It was at this time the daughter, never known to be very careful about her appearance, refused to put on a dress, to comb her hair, to brush her teeth, even to wash her face. She was happy living in filth, rebelling against the "perfect" mother who could not hold her husband.

When Kathy first came to see me alone, she confessed she was involved with drugs. She told me she would walk along the street, pick up a black man and tell him, "I'm going to be very rich when I'm twenty-one and inherit my grandmother's money. Will you take me to Harlem and get me some heroin?"

Kathy was referred to me by an internist who had been treating her mother for abdominal pains. The internist said, speaking over the telephone, "The mother is at her wit's end with Kathy. I can't understand how a girl with such a nice background and all that money is so scornful of her mother. She acts as though her mother doesn't exist. Her father, when he sees her, can't get anywhere with her, either. She defies them both, and seems to hate them. Maybe you can help her."

Kathy told me she never bothered to finish anything, that if she felt like playing truant from school she did, that she felt nothing was important, but she did keep her appointments with me—for two years. She obviously wanted help. She came at first only twice a week, then three times, then four. She admitted that the days she saw me she did not take drugs but on other days she had to have them. It was as though on the days I did not see her, I was rejecting her and she resorted to drugs as a solace.

We talked at great length of her feelings toward her mother. She confessed, "I *hate* my mother like poison. She pretends to be perfect. But she's a tyrant at heart. She wants to rule me just as she wanted to rule my father. I don't blame him for leaving her. Who could live with her?"

Kathy told, with some humor in her voice, how, when she was two years old, she hid for two days under a bed in one of their thirty guest rooms. Her parents thought she had been kidnapped and were frightened out of their senses. It was her way, at that time, of getting their attention, of saying, "I am here."

Although Kathy is a swinger in today's scene, she realizes she has deep emotional problems no drug can ease but will only intensify. She is trying to raise her self-esteem. She finished high school and is now attending art school; she brought in some of her paintings and I think she will make a fine commercial artist.

Here is a girl who got from her parents everything on this earth but love. And without love, she could not think much of herself, as her sloppy attire and uncleanliness showed when she first arrived in my office.

What is a mother really demanding of her child when she asks for perfection? Kathy's mother almost scrubbed her to death when she was a little girl. Kathy joked, "Mother even scrubbed all the natural oils off my skin."

Resenting such an unnatural demand for cleanliness, eventually there was only one thing for Kathy to do, literally revel in her body's filth and disorder as she expressed rebellion.

The persistent, endless "touching" by her mother of every sensitive spot on Kathy's body, must have aroused in the little girl a fear of sensual feelings she could not control. Such feelings had to be subdued, and out of fear of giving in to these feelings—in an opposite reaction—Kathy found the touch of her mother unpleasant. She said she would recoil from her mother's touch as though it were poison—"I hate my mother like poison," Kathy had said.

The fear of being poisoned comes very early in life, from the days of feeding by a mother. If there is too much hate in the air, the child will feel the mother wants to "poison" it through food. Anger is the psychic poison.

129

The mother who always must be "touching" the child, giving as rationalization that this is for the child's cleanliness, may create angry feelings in the child as it resists its homosexual feelings. The child naturally will respond sexually to the touch, for all children are sensual little beings, what Freud called "polymorphous perverse." They do not care who touches them—father, mother, uncle, maid, chauffeur, stranger—but only that they be petted, hugged, and caressed. This to them is love. The touch is the magic wand of childhood.

Kathy's mother was raised in Holland, a country noted for its clean, scrubbed look. She grew up no doubt with a mother who also overemphasized the importance of being clean. We have to be clean to be civilized, but like everything else, when the emphasis is excessive, beware the motive.

Kathy rebelled against the endless instructions for keeping clean: comb your hair, brush your teeth, wipe your mouth, have a bowel movement, clean your nails. One time after her mother sent her upstairs to take off her ragged blue jeans and put on a dress because there was company for supper, Kathy turned so violent she put her foot through the glass door that led to the terrace outside her bedroom.

In rebellion she did things she thought would most horrify her parents—she dated black men and took dope. She felt her parents did not care about her as a human being; that to them, she was only another possession. They did not let her make her own choices, do her own thing.

I am still working with Kathy, who has changed quite a bit. She dresses like other young women, takes a bath every day, visits the hairdresser once a week. She has been going for a year with a young man in law school and expects to marry him when he graduates. Her mother is now proud of her but in a different way. She recognizes that Kathy has the right to her own life. She no longer needs to control her "dirty little girl."

8.
THE YOUTH
WHO
ACTS OUT

THE BOY OR GIRL WHO STEALS, WHO TAKES DRUGS, WHO DEFIES his parents in action, is the one who is "acting out" his anger. Because he is driven by unconscious wishes, for the most part, no appeal to reason is likely to stop the acting-out.

If one looks closely, it can be seen that often a young person is caricaturing his parents. He learns to a great degree by imitating his mother and father, both consciously and unconsciously. His parents are his models, for better or worse.

But not the part of the parent that says, "Do as I say." Rather, the part of the parent that says, "Do as I do."

A parent may preach the highest morality but act recklessly and with abandon in his own life and the child will respond, not to the empty moralistic words, but to the recklessness and wantonness he sees before him.

A fifteen-year-old youth came to me because he was in trouble with the law. He belonged to a young gang that had planned and executed several robberies. They would burrow under large industrial plants to reach the room that contained the safe, dig an opening into the room, then crack the safe.

The boy's mother, a wealthy businesswoman, sent him to me for help. On the surface, before knowing the psychic facts, one would condemn the boy as a delinquent.

131

The story came out, through the boy, that his father had been an alcoholic who had refused to work, insisting the mother support him. He was also a thief, for, when eventually he walked out on wife and son, he stole from her money and jewelry worth thousands of dollars. She did not prosecute because she believed she was well rid of him.

The boy had become a thief just like his father, the only image of "man" in his life. To the boy, there was something daring and glamorous (and also "masculine") about the criminal act. Do not we all enjoy the suspense movie in which thieves plot crimes, do not we agonize with the thieves as they plan and carry out the crimes, fearing they will get caught, wanting them to get away free? The impulse to steal comes from childhood—children feel everything in the world is theirs for the taking.

The fact that this youth's mother had not prosecuted his father told the boy, in a sense, she was condoning the robbery and would not prosecute her son, should he be caught in a similar act. In spite of her wasting little time informing her son what a "thief" and "bum" his father had been, all the while insisting the son be "good" and "law-abiding," the boy responded to the feelings in the air, not to the words she mouthed. She had married a "thief" and a "bum" and that was proof enough for her son she really admired such a man.

The stealing of cars, to the unconscious, is the stealing of power, and power, in the unconscious, is the possession of a phallus. The car—fast, powerful, able to kill—has often been compared, psychoanalytically speaking, to the penis.

The movie *Bonnie and Clyde* depicts a young couple who stole cars, then held up banks, and killed. All the while they were trying to get sadistic sexual satisfaction from the thrills of stealing and killing. The young man was impotent and the young woman was acting out her wish to be a man. This was clearly shown in the dramatic film presentation.

We might conjecture from what little we know of their backgrounds that both Bonnie and Clyde were acting out intense fury at their parents, a fury carried from childhood. In the beginning of the movie, Bonnie is seen as desperate to leave her mother and a life that bores her. Boredom is usually a manifestation of repressed anger. Clyde's impotence with Bonnie and his need to murder are clear signs of a childish rage that could not be contained.

Gambling is another activity in which unconscious sexual excitement is sought, although in a masochistic way, as the late Dr. Edmund Bergler, psychoanalyst, pointed out in his book, *The Psychology of Gambling*. He maintained that the compulsive gambler unconsciously does not want to win, that his satisfaction comes in taking a beating through the loss of money.

The child who steals is saying many things to his parents and to society. On one level he is making a plea for love and attention. He is saying he does not care enough about himself or his parents to observe the laws. He is asking that he be helped to raise his self-esteem.

He is also telling of great rage at his parents, a rage that keeps him from obeying them. He has given up on receiving their love, he believes they have none to give, and therefore he can do nothing to earn it. He has to feel someone cares for him before he will cease his rebellion.

The young person who is a pathological liar usually has deep emotional conflicts. He is driven by fantasies that make him feel reality has few rewards. The pathological liar will even lie to the therapist and therefore is difficult to treat. I try to praise such a youngster for his honest words and deeds,

133

hoping he will eventually face up to the deception and hypocrisy in which he engages and gradually come to understand the reason for his psychological dependence on such a false pattern of behavior.

The young person who tells lies may be afraid of telling the truth. He may fear to show himself up as a coward or thief (children sometimes steal from their mothers' purses). He knows he will get punished if he is caught in a lie, but the greater fear is the truth, so he believes. He has to be helped to know that only the truth sets him free, as the Bible says.

The lies most dangerous are those one has to tell the self. One young man of seventeen was convinced his mother had thrown his father out of the house when he was seven. He had always blamed her because his father was not on the scene. And the blame took the form of continual rebellious acts and hostility on his part. In this fashion he managed to wreak his "revenge" upon her.

It was a shock to him one day when his mother confessed that she had asked his father to leave after she discovered he was having an affair with the woman next door. The reason for her silence was rooted in the desire to shield her son from the knowledge—which she felt would be a severe psychological blow to him.

The youth said in wonder, "I guess I always knew this but wanted to blame you. Somehow it made my life easier. I didn't want to face the thought that my father didn't think enough of me and you to keep faithful."

Children from broken homes often have emotional problems. Yet, such problems can be avoided. If a child is helped to understand that separation of his parents is essential for their happiness, as well as his own, he can adjust to a broken home.

The child should be allowed to see parents who are separated whenever he wishes. He should not be forced to visit one or the other parent if he feels uncomfortable or frighten.

A twelve-year-old girl confessed to me about her divorc. father, "I really don't like seeing him. He scares me. Bu Mama gets mad at me if I don't visit Daddy once a month."

I called up her mother, reported her daughter's reaction. I suggested she refrain from insisting that the girl visit her father but see him only when she felt like it.

Parents who are separated must beware of a child playing one against the other for monetary or other gain. Children can be the most adept emotional manipulators in the world, if allowed free rein.

Separated parents should also be careful not to instill poisonous feelings in the child about the absent mate. They may blame each other in privacy if they wish but when they are with the child they should try to create a feeling in him that he has a dependable mother and father. He should feel he belongs to both even though they may live apart. He should believe his parents have made a choice for which he is in no way responsible and they will guide and protect and love him even though they cannot get along with each other any longer. In this fashion they can help him adjust emotionally to the disruption of the normal family existence which is his birthright, and excessive hostility toward one or both parents— with its accompanying psychic traumas—will be largely avoided.

With the alarming increase in divorces, the role of the stepparent has become very important. It takes time for a child to accept and trust a stepparent, the intruder in his family. As one little boy said defiantly to his new stepmother, "You're not my mother! You're only my father's second wife."

She tried to reassure him. "I don't want to take your mother's place. I'm just an additional mother, if you should ever want one."

135

She knew she would need time for him to trust and like her. Meanwhile, she was content to make him aware that she liked him, not in a gesture of false friendship but for the nice qualities he possessed.

Sometimes acting-out will occur when the young person has to separate from his parents and does not know how to handle what psychiatrists call "separation anxiety." This may strike at any time of his life from the day of birth on, whenever he becomes separated from his mother for any length of time. The first separation in our lives occurs with the cutting of the umbilical cord. Up to then, the baby has had the complete shelter of his mother's body, which has housed and fed him. Now he is on his own. He has to cry to signal when he is hungry or when his diaper is wet. Most mothers, through attention and love, help babies master this first separation anxiety.

Dr. D. W. Winnicott, in his book *Mother And Child,* points to the importance to the child during the period of first separation from the mother, of what he calls a "transitional object." This may be a teddy bear, a blanket, the mother's handkerchief or woolen scarf. Says Dr. Winnicott, "It is not the object itself, of course, that is transitional; it represents the infant's transition from a state of being merged with the mother to a state of being in relation to the mother as something outside and separate."

From the infant's point of view, this first object was created out of his imagination, says Dr. Winnicott, "and it does seem that we have to admit that in the case of every infant the world has to be created anew. The world as it presents itself is of no meaning to the newly developing human being unless it is created as well as discovered."

When the mother or other person on whom the infant is dependent is absent there is no immediate change, owing to the

136

fact that the infant has an internal version of the mother which remains alive for a certain length of time, he says. If, however, the mother is absent for a long period of time, the internal version fades, and the "transitional objects" become meaningless. "What we see now is an infant who must be nursed or fed and who, if left alone, tends to go over into exciting activities with sensuous gratification," he explains. What is lost is the whole intermediate area of affectionate contact.

When, at a later stage, a child feels abandoned and becomes unable to play and display or accept deep affection, there may be compulsive erotic activities. Stealing by deprived children can be said to be part of the search for the transitional object, lost through the death or fading of the internalized version of the mother, Dr. Winnicott maintains. Such a child is bound to be an angry child, for anger follows on the heels of abandonment.

Eventually children give up these transitional objects, "like old soldiers the objects simply fade away."

He further states that, as a child psychiatrist, when he sees children, he finds to his surprise they easily remember the very early objects to which they were attached, when they talk about themselves and their dreams. He warns it is distressing for children not only when the object is lost, as sometimes happens by accident, but when a parent with a lack of understanding takes away the teddy bear or furry rabbit and tucks it in the crib with a new baby. Hostility will develop when transitional objects are taken away unfeelingly—the child loses a psychic prop and feels a different form of betrayal or abandonment as another seed of hate is sown.

It is interesting how many young people take a cherished stuffed animal to boarding school or college when they leave home. It is their security blanket, so to speak.

The first day of school, when a child must go off on his

own, may produce separation anxiety. Most children encouraged by parents and teachers to take this first big step toward independence do so easily. The child who is unable to accept the step, who whimpers for his mother, who hates school, may need assistance to overcome his anxiety.

When a youth goes off to boarding school or college, the anxiety may become apparent once more. He moves out of his home, out of the privacy of his room, away from most of his beloved possessions. He loses the shelter, the supervision, and the attention he got at home.

The young person who is emotionally secure may feel lonely at times at college but he will soon assume a life of his own, in preparation for moving entirely away from his mother and father. He will look forward to visits home and enjoy his vacations, but he also welcomes the return to college and his classmates.

But if a boy or girl has been either too anxious to leave home, or does not want to leave home at all, he may have traumatic experiences at college. The youth who cannot wait to escape his mother and father may find there is no substitute for the comforts and amenities of home. The one reluctant to leave home may find he is unable to deal with his separation anxiety and has to drop out of college. Or he may try to stick it out even though his anxiety is intense and the pressures of collegiate life heavy. Such a young person may be unable to study, he may get depressed and withdrawn, cut classes, take to drugs—all of this reflecting his anger at his parent whom he blames for forcing him to leave home before he is ready for such an important change.

Today many colleges and universities have mental health services. They recognize the importance of providing psychological help to youth in conflict.

Another form of acting-out is shown by the girl who becomes pregnant without being married. In spite of the fact that some of our leading movie actresses announce publicly they are pregnant but do not intend to marry the father of their baby, to get married and provide a baby with a father is still considered the thing to do. From what we know of emotional security, it is best achieved with two parents.

Inside every unwed mother seethes a very angry little girl. She is a little girl who unconsciously is taking her father away from her mother. She is an angry girl rebelling against all her mother stands for.

The young woman who allows herself to get pregnant at a time of life when parents, as a rule, ask her not to get involved sexually before she is married is rebelling in rage against her parents, no matter how loudly she protests she has become pregnant for love of a young man. If she loved him, she would marry him. She knows the deepest hurt she can inflict on her parents, especially her mother, is to get pregnant although unwed. I am speaking here of the many girls who actually "invite" their pregnancy—consciously or unconsciously—in a twisted form of revenge against their parents for dominating their activities, smothering their identity, undue interference in dating and other similar complaints.

One sixteen-year-old girl sent to me by her doctor was pregnant and not married. She had told her physician when he announced she was pregnant, "I'll have to kill myself."

She did not know the father because she had been promiscuous and it could have been any one of four young men. During therapy, she revealed that her mother had taken care of her ever since her father left home when she was six. As an only child, she had received the brunt of her mother's love and concern, in this case, overconcern. Her mother was obsessed with cleanliness. She would daily inspect and clean her daughter's every orifice—ears, nose, mouth, anus, vagina.

139

"At bedtime the Q-tips came out and I was poked everywhere," the daughter told me. "Mother sometimes even looked for lice in my hair. I always *hated* being poked. But she insisted on doing it until I was almost fifteen."

She got even with her mother when she was "poked" in the most basic way of all, a way that made her pregnant.

So serious is the problem of unwed mothers in New York city schools that recently the Department of Health sent instructions to all elementary and secondary schools on what to do if a pregnant student went into labor or gave birth while in school. This action was prompted by the school system's new policy, initiated in the fall of 1969, of encouraging pregnant girls to remain in school and continue their education as long as possible. The schools in 1969 reported 2,487 pregnancies among unmarried girls in the seventh to twelfth grades. This was nearly double the figure of eight years ago.

Young girls who are promiscuous are acting out their rebellion against their parents for real or imagined hurts and derelictions, for the withholding of love and affection, for neglect or abandonment—and against a society they view as depraved, cynical, and uncaring. To make matters worse, society strikes a blow against women by being more tolerant, during adolescence and later, of the sexual adventures of young men.

The daughter of a lawyer took promiscuity as a way of showing her anger at parents during her last year in high school. Lila would steal home early in the morning, let herself into her parents' house with her own key after spending several hours in a hotel room with strange men she picked up at a bar. She was taking the pill on the sly so she did not worry about pregnancy. She was not a drug addict but drank to excess.

On the surface Lila was a friendly girl, seemingly controlled and disciplined. She had large gray eyes, long auburn

140

hair coiled on top of her head to make her look older, and a rounded, feminine figure.

When she first saw Rusty, she said in relief, "I'm glad you don't have a cat. I hate cats!"

Several sessions later, after I knew more abou. her, I asked why she disliked cats so intensely.

"My mother's a cat," she said.

"Why do you say that?"

"She's always making catty remarks, and she sneaks up on me like a cat when I least expect it."

I thought of Lila sneaking in to her house every night as her parents slept, but said nothing. I did not want to put her on the defensive. In time, she would see herself more clearly.

In sudden wrath she said, "And my father's a cat, too. A tomcat!"

"What do you mean?"

"He's got no more morals than an alley cat," she said contemptuously. "He boasts of sleeping with his secretary, his manicurist, and God knows what other whore."

"He tells you this?" I was surprised a father would confide his secret life to a young daughter.

"He tells my mother, and then she tells me."

"Why do you think she tells you?" I could understand a wife's feeling bereft and angry because of her husband's promiscuity, but asking her young daughter to share her misery is putting too great a burden on the daughter.

Lila shrugged her shoulders. "I guess because we've always been close. I am her best friend. She tells me everything."

"There are some things a mother would be wise not to tell her daughter," I suggested.

Her eyes widened in surprise. "You think I shouldn't know the facts of life?"

141

"I think there are times parents should keep their troubles to themselves," I said firmly.

She was uncertain as to how to take this. She looked at me, puzzled. Finally she said, "I hate him on my own, anyhow. How my mother feels makes no difference to me."

"I would think you love him very much and can't understand how he could do such a thing to your mother and you," I said quietly.

Her eyes suddenly filled with tears and she reached for a facial tissue on my desk.

After drying her eyes, she said, "He gives me everything I could possibly want. When my set of matched golf clubs was stolen last week from my convertible Cadillac, he immediately ordered another set. I have all the clothes I need. I have three fur coats. And yet I'm miserable."

"Your actions show that," I said. "No young woman who was happy would get drunk at bars, pick up strange men and sleep with them in hotel rooms, then creep home in guilt."

"Why do I do it?" she wailed. "I hate myself for it."

"For one thing, you want to get even with your father," I said. "Aren't you copying exactly what you accuse him of doing? Sleeping around?"

"That never occurred to me," she replied. "This is my revenge, isn't it?"

"Would your mother ever do a thing like that?" I asked.

"Never!" There was horror in her voice. "Mother is a lady."

"And you are bent on destroying your image of yourself as a lady."

She was now sobbing, "How can he do this to me?"

"He isn't doing it to you, but to your mother," I said. "It is really her problem, not yours. And if she wants revenge, she will get it in her own way."

This mother was unconsciously asking her daughter to avenge her, otherwise she never would have told Lila of her father's infidelity. She probably wanted sympathy but she had other motives, too, ones of which she may not have been aware when she "squealed" on her errant husband.

The acting-out of young people is caused by many motivating events and circumstances in their lives. It would be oversimplifying the truth to attribute it to any one. But in general we can be sure that when youth is delinquent or acts with abandon in any extreme way, fury at parents surges underneath.

The use of obscenity by young people is another way of acting out defiance of parents.

"Why do you use four-letter words so much?" I asked one boy of sixteen, whose every other word was an obscenity.

"Just to get grown-ups mad," he said, grinning. "We don't like grown-ups. We want a world of our own."

"How do you feel about me?" I asked.

"Oh, you're just a shrink," he said, dismissing me as less than a grown-up.

One mother went into hysterics when her seven-year-old daughter burst into the house in tears and said, "I met Jimmy on the street," Jimmy was the next-door neighbor's fifteen-year-old son, "and I asked him what time it was because you told me not to be late, and he said, 'Tell your mother to go screw herself.' "

The little girl had been frightened of the word, not knowing exactly what it meant but sensing it was a word she should not hear. The neighbor's son was a rebellious youth, according to the little girl's mother, always in trouble for misbehaving.

The child who feels emotionally secure will not be alarmed by the obscene words when he hears them nor will he feel in need of using them to shock others.

143

A young man of eighteen while in therapy with me went to work during the Christmas holidays in the necktie section of a department store.

I cautioned him, knowing he was short of temper, "Remember that you need a lot of patience to deal with Christmas shoppers."

"I'll try," he muttered.

At his next session, two days later, he walked in sheepishly, slumped in the chair dejectedly.

"What's the matter?" I asked, knowing well what the matter was.

"I lasted five hours," he confessed.

"What happened?"

"Three women came over to the counter and didn't buy anything after looking for twenty minutes apiece. The fourth was my undoing. She was big and fat and she picked up one tie after another and threw it down, mumbling to herself, 'My husband would like this one,' then, 'No, I guess he wouldn't.' Finally, in desperation, I said, 'Madam, which tie do you want? I have to go out for lunch.'

" 'Don't rush me, young man!' she snapped. 'I'll take all the time I want to make up my mind and you'll stand right there until I'm ready!' "

He fell quiet, as though the story were finished.

"Well?" I asked, trying to hide a smile, for I could guess his reaction.

"Well, what?" He was fencing.

"What did you say to her?"

He bit his lips, then admitted, "I said to her, quote, 'Lady, go screw.' "

"And what did she do?"

"She turned purple and said, 'Where is the section manager?' And I pointed to where he stood, in plain view, and said, 'Right over there, Madam.' "

"And so you got fired," I said.

"And so I got fired," he repeated.

From what he told me of this customer, she sounded very much like his own mother who had difficulty making up her mind and who was also quite plump.

"Did the woman remind you of anyone?" I asked.

He frowned, thinking, then shook his head. "No."

"Who do you know who is also plump and who has trouble reaching decisions?" I asked. "Someone about whom you have complained here endlessly that she never knows what she wants."

"Oh!" Sudden awareness gleamed in his eyes. "You mean my mother!"

"Doesn't it strike you as interesting that you reacted so violently to a strange woman who obviously was confused as to which tie her husband would like?" I asked.

"You mean I reacted to her that way because she was like my mother?" He sounded incredulous.

"I think so," I said. "Otherwise you could have accepted the woman's indecision as somewhat pathetic and simply shrugged your shoulders and given her all the time in the world to make up her mind."

"I was hungry!" he complained.

"That's rationalization," I told him. "It wouldn't have hurt you to have waited five or ten minutes longer to eat. Besides, you're always complaining you're too fat."

"You really think that's why I exploded at the old bag—because she reminded me of my mother?" he said in wonder.

"Think about it," I said. "All I know is what I've heard you say about your mother."

145

The projection onto strangers of a rage whose target is really a parent is a familiar psychological defense. Prejudice is explained by the psychic process known as "projection." Children are especially adept at the use of projection since their powers of reason are not fully developed.

An obscene gesture was used as defiance by an eighteen-year-old student at a local college, sent to me by the college for diagnosis. He had been expelled for exhibitionism.

I asked what he had done. He was reluctant to discuss it, saying nervously, "Didn't they tell you?"

"They said merely that you had created quite a scene."

"I guess I did," he admitted.

"What did you do?" I wondered if he had suddenly hurled off all his clothes and plunged naked into a campus pool. Or wandered nude around the dormitory.

"I'd better tell," he said, as though confessing to a murder. "As they were taking the class photograph for the yearbook, at the very moment the camera clicked, I unzipped my fly and exposed myself."

It was difficult for me to hide a smile, for this was one of of the most imaginative, expressive, direct ways of indicating anger that I had ever come across. But I was there to help him, not to be amused.

"Don't you want to graduate from college?" I asked. He was in his freshman year.

"I'll never make it," he muttered.

"Not if you keep breaking rules," I said.

"There's no rule against unzipping your fly when your picture is being taken," he insisted.

"Not a college rule, but a rule society has set," I pointed out. "If a man did that on the street, he would be arrested."

"That's a very prudish way of looking at life," he objected.

146

"It's worked for thousands of years," I said. "There would be far more disorder in our streets without such a law."

Youth is quick to demand change without taking into account the consequences. Youth forgets that over the centuries, painfully, sometimes violently, man has forged customs and laws that work for the greatest good of the greatest number. Sometimes these customs and laws are wrong, but they are changed most easily by discussion and thoughtful action, not by violence or rebellion, which always antagonizes those in favor of the status quo so much that they refuse any change.

I asked this young man, "Why did you feel the need to expose yourself at the very moment the photo was taken?"

"I was telling the college authorities what I thought of them," he answered.

"Why didn't you tell them directly?" I asked.

"They wouldn't listen," was his reply.

"Did you try?"

"No," he admitted.

"Exactly what is it you want to tell them?"

"I don't like the courses I have to take," he said.

"Can't you talk this over with your professors or guidance counselor?"

He was silent.

"What's the matter?" I asked, suspecting he was troubled by something that had gone unmentioned.

"I don't dare talk to them," he said. "My father would get furious if I changed my major. He wants me to take business administration."

I realized, then, that the defiance was not at the university but at the father who insisted he take certain courses. The father was the one at whom this student was thumbing his penis, so to speak.

"What do you want to major in?" I asked.

"Architecture," he said emphatically. "But my father calls that a dreamer's profession. He wants me to earn money quickly, to run his business when I graduate."

Here again a parent was not letting a young person make his own decisions, but saying, "Papa knows best," and sometimes papa does not know best. This youth, in desperation, was expressing a deep anger at his father for stifling his creativity, for forcing him into a mold he hated.

"Do you mind if I see your father and try to help him understand what you would like to do?" I asked.

A look of sheer joy came over his face. "I'd be so grateful," he said. "I can't get anywhere with him. Maybe you can, since you're a psychiatrist."

I telephoned his father. He came to see me and I explained why the incident at college had happened. The father, far from being the tyrant I expected, appeared to be a rather meek, mild-mannered man, confused by the turn of events.

"I had no idea Bruce felt this way," he told me apologetically. "I would like him to run my business after I retire. But if he feels very strongly about becoming an architect, I certainly would put up no barrier to his changing courses."

"Tell him that," I suggested. "And then call the university and explain why you think your son was rebelling. I am sure they will be sympathetic and take him back."

The university agreed to do this if Bruce accepted the help of the psychiatrist on the campus, which I considered a good idea. Bruce was willing to do so. I have heard no further from him and I believe some day he will make his mark as an architect. No doubt the college psychiatrist over the months or years will help Bruce understand why his rage at his father took the form of exhibitionism—a rather bizarre way to express defiance but one certainly guaranteed to shock.

Another youth, sixteen years old, had been acting-out at college during his first year away from home by taking drugs and traveling with a rather wild set. He was enjoying a new freedom away from a home in which he had been brought up strictly.

His mother and father came to see me to ask my advice about what to do. His father explained, "We want to send Jerry to a very strict boys' school in England, set in the hills miles from the nearest city. He goes crazy with the slightest bit of freedom and we have to protect him."

"Wouldn't it be better to let him find out for himself what he should or should not do?" I said. "He has had a very conventional upbringing, from what you tell me. If you send him to a school miles from the nearest city, he may resent it and rebel in a far more serious way."

"More serious than taking drugs and sleeping with sluts?" demanded the father.

"This is a phase many young men go through. It does not mean they will continue," I said. "He may be merely sowing wild oats."

This the parents did not want to hear. They left my office shaking their heads sadly, saying they could not follow my advice but were going to send their son abroad. I could not halt their need to punish him.

The so-called "spoiled" child (the word "spoiled" is an apt one, for an indulged child's psyche may, indeed, be spoiled) may draw sympathy from psychiatrists but only anger, as a rule, from adults when he grows older and refuses to become unspoiled. There are many wealthy young people who in their early years are given great freedom, much money, but little supervision, and left to their own devices. When the rebellious time of adolescence arrives, parents expect them to "straighten up and fly right," only to find that their grown sons and daughters resent any limits, any commands, any sudden supervision.

Such parents complain, "This is the way my child repays me, after all the gifts I have lavished on him, all I have done for him, all the love I have bestowed upon him."

No parent believes he does not love a child. I have never heard a parent say, "I hate my child." He may dislike certain characteristics of the child, or certain patterns of behavior, but he will not say, as children do about a parent, "I hate him," even though there are times a youngster will try the spirit of the most permissive parent. If you examine the situation thoroughly you are apt to find the parent has had some role in causing his child's rebellious behavior.

A nineteen-year-old youth who had been having violent arguments with his father was sent to me by the family physician. The father wanted to commit his son to a mental hospital because he thought his son was insane.

"He thinks I'm nuts," said the young man, a blond, rather plump but pleasant looking youth.

"Why does your father think that?" I asked.

"Because I sleep late in the morning, cut classes when I feel like it, don't care whether I graduate from college. He says all I want to do is raise hell at night. He thinks I'm no good. All I ask is that he let me be."

He told me that he would get a $2 million trust fund left him by his grandmother within a month.

"And I don't want to touch that trust," he said.

"Why not?" Usually young people cannot wait to get their hands on money.

"The old man is already telling me how to invest it."

"Are you afraid he will take it away from you?"

"I don't know why he would. He's got millions of his

own. It's just that I don't want to be told what to do with it."

"Even if your father wants to show you how to invest it wisely?" I could understand that the father might feel his son would throw the money away.

"I'm sick of his suddenly telling me what to do after years of paying no attention to me. I'd rather let the money just sit in the trust."

In an interview with the father, I got the picture of a parent who had been too permissive in some areas, too protective in others—a frequent pattern with parents. He had indulged his son as far as material possessions were concerned and allowed him to live a carefree, pleasure-seeking life. He told me incidents that showed his son had difficulty restraining his rebellious impulses. One particular occasion, in fact, he got into a brawl in a bar and severely beat up another youth. Another time he was arrested for drunken driving. The father, therefore, did not want his son to be undisciplined about the money to which he would fall heir.

"Do you think your son would accept psychiatric help?" I asked.

"He might. Why don't you suggest it? I'd be glad to pay for it."

The next time I saw the young man I said, "Your father seems to think you are irresponsible and would throw away the money. Do you think you would go to a psychiatrist in your college town?"

He shrugged his shoulders, undoubtedly knowing he needed one. "Why not? Although it's my old man who needs help."

His final words to me were, "Thank you, Doctor Stevens. Maybe someday I'll understand my father."

My goodbye words were, "As you understand yourself, Robert."

The subject of money is larded with emotional overtones in the relationship between parent and child. Money can be used unwisely for many purposes including a bribe for love, a way out of spending time with a child and a way of punishing or controlling a child. Too often such indiscriminate disposing of money, particularly when used as a substitute for parental love, attention, and affection, only breeds resentment and rebellion in the youthful recipient.

I see so many young people given extravagant allowances who do not know how to spend wisely. For one thing, they have not been taught the value of money. They feel no responsibility for money they have not earned. Also, they often take out their anger at a parent by flinging away money he has given them, as though symbolically flinging away the parent.

At the other extreme, some parents are miserly with money. A sixteen-year-old girl told me, tears in her eyes, "I hate to ask my father for a cent because he makes me feel like a criminal for asking—as if I don't deserve it."

Money is closely tied to self-esteem. Parents must be careful not to toss money in scorn at a youngster for then he will feel degraded. Money should be respected as a sign of earning power and for what it can purchase to make life comfortable, not used destructively.

A word, perhaps, should be said about the therapist's acting-out. The good therapist never gets emotionally involved with a patient. He empathizes with him, but in order to help the therapist must maintain an emotional distance between himself and the patient. He must never become physically involved with the patient. This is the unwritten law of the profession.

Freud summarized a good analyst in these words:

What is given to the patient should, indeed, never be a spontaneous effect [emotion] but always consciously allotted, and then more or less of it as the need may arise. Occasionally a great deal, but never from one's own unconscious. This I should regard as the formula. In other words, one must always recognize one's counter transference [feelings for the patient] and rise above it, only then is one free oneself. To give someone too little because one loves him too much is being unjust to the patient and a technical error.

Prevention of juvenile delinquency has been one of my greatest interests. I am Director of Psychiatry for the National Society for the Prevention of Juvenile Delinquency. The society's goal is to reduce juvenile delinquency through education of the public and psychotherapy of the child and parents when indicated.

I have recommended in talks throughout the nation that every school have a psychiatrist on its staff to help recognize and treat the symptoms that develop into delinquency. A psychiatrist can often discover the reasons why a child "goes wrong," before he becomes so angry that he erupts into a full-fledged delinquent.

The reasons may not always be emotional. One twelve-year-old child came to me because he was inattentive in school and punished frequently for being "lazy." I sent him for a physical checkup, sensing there might be something physically wrong, and found he had low blood pressure. He was treated for that and immediately became interested in his studies, and thereafter was not a problem pupil in school.

I think the following six points are most important in the prevention of delinquency:

(1) Immediate therapy for the overly aggressive, restless, or sensitive child, particularly if sleep disturbances are present.

(2) Early recognition of specific intellectual malfunctioning, such as reading disabilities and dysphasias, and then the instituting of remedial teaching. If the defect is of such a nature that it cannot be corrected, there should be placement in a special class or individual instruction.

(3) Placement of adolescents who are intellectually and/or emotionally unsuited for classroom work into a work situation or apprenticeship program.

(4) Psychotherapy for the sensitive, intelligent, and idealistic adolescent who develops a contempt for society.

(5) Aid for parents whose own problems, be they psychological or financial, interfere and frustrate the legitimate needs and aspirations of the child.

(6) Increased participation of the adolescent in adult social life, where he can identify with responsible adults and adopt adult behavior patterns.

Here is a list of danger signals that can alert parents to seek professional help:

(1) Excessive aggressiveness on the part of a child or adolescent.

(2) Restlessness and sensitivity, which may be symptoms of anxiety and can lead to drug addiction and a life of crime to support the narcotics habit.

(3) Sleep disturbances, which indicate anxiety.

(4) School problems, such as lack of concentration, reading difficulties and abnormal behavior in class, whether it be a need to be the "class clown," or disruptive and destructive, or shy and depressed.

(5) Deterioration of academic performance with the onset of adolescence.

(6) Lack of communication between parents and children to an extreme degree.

154

(7) Inferiority complex in relation to family and surroundings which may produce "gang leaders" because of the youngster's desire to overcome insecurity and lack of confidence.

While juvenile delinquency usually is found in the teenager, the symptoms leading to it can be discovered at earlier ages. Parents who see symptoms should seek psychiatric help for the child.

Another potential delinquent is the child denied enough adult company. Boys, who sometimes rarely see their fathers, live in an almost completely woman-dominated world, and may suffer from this more than girls. Sometimes teachers are of little help, for usually the teacher will look on both the child who disrupts the class and the one who daydreams as a threat to his authority. He may use force, ridicule, or threats to change the child. This is one reason I advocate a psychiatrist for every school. He can help teachers, as well as pupils and parents.

I have never forgotten my discussion with a nine-year-old boy referred to me because of disruptive behavior in school.

"Why were you asked to come here?" I queried.

"Because I am bad," replied the boy.

"Do you want to be bad?" I asked.

"No, I want to be good," he said.

"What would you have to do to be good?"

"Sit quietly in class and pay attention to the teacher."

"You know what to do to be good," I said. "Then why aren't you good?"

The youngster gave me a puzzled stare. "I don't know. I just can't help it."

He was absolutely correct. He could not help it. Therapy enabled him to become a model student as in my office he gave vent to some of his feelings about the school and his parents, feelings he had tried to deny in his aggressive behavior at school. The problem in his case was rooted in his resentment at being ignored by his parents who were too much caught up in their own social and business pursuits. His behavior tantrums were a pathetic attempt to gain attention, to make his folks more aware of him.

Again, it is interesting to see how children will imitate parents. A seven-year-old boy was referred to me because of restless and exuberant behavior in school. He was of high intelligence, friendly and charming, but a bundle of uncontrolled energy. When questioned whether anyone in the family had shown similar traits, his mother said, "Yes, I was very much like him. My nickname as a child was 'Lightning.' " She had become a dancing instructor and found an acceptable outlet for her own energy, but the school had not afforded her son enough activity so his energy could be contained or properly channeled.

The child or young person who eats continually so that he becomes fat and the object of ridicule by family and friends is also acting out. The fat child is an angry or unhappy child. He overeats because of emotional needs, the victim of what has been so aptly named "hidden hunger." Children and young people should not be forced to diet, for they need variety in their food. Rather, they should get help for the conflicts driving them to overeat.

Food is a great source of conflict between the angry child and his parent. It is the child's first battleground. He learns early in life he can make his mother furious by refusing to eat. If he will not eat but starves to death and dies it is her fault, and he can punish her unmercifully by turning away from food.

During adolescence girls and boys tend to eat as a sublimation for giving in to their aroused sexual desire. If they eat too much, this too can worry a parent.

156

A fourteen-year-old girl walked into my office almost filling the door as she entered. She told me she weighed 180 pounds.

"Do you like being so plump?" I asked her.

She tossed her head angrily. "It makes my mother furious and I couldn't be happier!" she said.

"Why are you happy when she is angry?" I asked.

"Because she likes to make me angry," she replied.

"In what way?"

"She's always trying to keep me from eating. She won't buy cakes or pies or ice cream because she thinks they'll put weight on me. So I go to the store and eat them there. Who does she think she's fooling?"

As it turned out, this girl had a legitimate reason to be angry. Her father had walked out of the family home a year before and had not been heard from since, except through checks he sent intermittently for support. The mother did nothing but complain endlessly about her fate in life. She refused to let her daughter go out on dates, even to the movies with a boy. And her daughter was showing her resentment by stuffing herself with food (symbolically devouring her devouring mother, in a sense).

Anger will out, one way or another. One young person will overeat, another starve himself so he becomes little more than skin and bones. One youth will drive his car recklessly all over the nation, another will withdraw to the privacy of his bedroom and refuse to move out of it. One girl will become promiscuous, another will not let a boy even hold her hand.

The path each troubled youngster takes depends on the many experiences in his life from the day he is born and what he sees happening before his eyes in his home as he grows up.

Time and time again the hangups of youngsters, their

157

acting out, their antisocial behavior, are a conscious or unconscious reaction to conflicts within the family—conflicts that
breed hatred for parents and vengeful acts initiated directly or
indirectly against them.

9.
THE YOUTH
WHO
WITHDRAWS

IN CONTRAST TO THE YOUTH WHO ACTS OUT HIS ANGER IS
the one who becomes withdrawn. He keeps himself from ac-
tively expressing how he feels, turning his rage inward. We
all do this to some extent but the withdrawn young person
does so to an unrealistic degree as he tries to retreat from what
he believes to be a painful reality.

The extreme example of withdrawal can be seen in the
schizophrenic child, in particular the catatonic child. Such
a child will not move a muscle but holds himself stonily rigid
lest he burst forth in murderous violence.

Opinions of psychiatrists vary with respect to the cause
of schizophrenia and how it should be treated. Some believe
there may be various kinds of schizophrenia, just as there are
various types of viruses and cancers.

There are psychiatrists who maintain that everyone who
does not conform to the reality of the outer world is schizophrenic. I knew one psychiatrist at Bellevue Hospital who
called every youngster schizophrenic even when there was the
possibility he was only borderline. I feel we should be more
flexible about diagnosis.

In the popular mind, schizophrenia, once called "juvenile
insanity" because it appeared in so many young people, is

associated with "split personality." Instead of feeling integrated and in harmony with himself, the person feels split in two or pulled in many directions.

There are youths who possess schizophrenic qualities even though they may not conform to the medical diagnosis of schizophrenia, as I pointed out about Susan Atkins and Charles Manson. Their mental apparatus has not completely broken down, as in the cases of those whose talk is pure gibberish, who are incapable of complete sentences or thoughts. But the thinking of an Atkins or a Manson is paranoid (unduly suspicious of others) and irrational much of the time.

Then there are those youths who exhibit no schizophrenic qualities but who show their withdrawal in other ways. One is the underachiever in school. He may be held prisoner by his emotional chains so that he does not have the energy or will to learn.

A recent headline in *The New York Times* read: "WHY PUPILS DON'T LEARN HELD MYSTERY."

The newspaper story went on to say that despite the great amount of money invested in special teaching programs in New York City "nobody" knew why certain children, especially those in poverty areas, were not profiting from the educational program.

"We have been spending a great deal of money on solutions which have little relation to causes," said Dr. Nathan Brown, Acting Superintendent of Schools.

But psychiatrists know the causes. They know that an emotionally troubled child often *will not* learn. He is too psychically confused to learn no matter what inducements the school offers.

This is not to say that poverty should not be abolished, or that children living in slum areas do not have an additional strike against them. It must be remembered that children who live in slum areas may have mothers and fathers who are emotionally disturbed and pass on the disturbances to the child. However, many children of wealthy parents are every bit as emotionally sick as any child of the slums. Emotions are the great leveler.

Occasionally a youngster from a wealthy family will commit suicide, hurling himself from the window of the luxurious apartment in which he lives or taking an overdose of his parents' sleeping pills. Readers of his death in a newspaper will comment in amazement, "This young person had everything!" meaning money and a lavish home. But money and a lavish home are *not* everything. There must be love and understanding in that lavish home. And there is often love and understanding in the slum home, or everyone born in the slums would be emotionally sick—and this is not true.

The happiest baby I ever saw slept in a crib in the bathtub of his parents' two-room apartment. His father, a young doctor just starting in practice, could afford only the one large living room in which he and his wife slept. But they gave the baby love and care and he thrived emotionally even though his bedroom was the bathtub.

Affluence is not the answer to the anger and rage of our young. A child must have love and security in his heart.

Many a young person from a wealthy home has been brought to my office because he has a learning problem. As I probe the reasons for his learning disabilities, I see the symptoms of underlying disorders that prevent him from normal achievement in academic work. There are always symptoms revealing that *a child does not want to succeed in his work.*

The symptoms most frequently encountered are depression, anxiety, and hyperactivity. The underlying disorder then has to be determined. Intellectual impairment may be caused

161

by minimal brain damage and strephosymbolia, classified as neurological, although this is the exception rather than the rule. Psychological conflicts, for the most part, keep our youth from learning. And these conflicts are frequently rooted in a malfunctioning of parent-child relationships that spur the development of anger and hostility on the youthful side of that coin.

I am often surprised by how well children with severe psychological conflicts function academically. When you learn the extent of their psychic disturbances, you wonder how they study at all.

Additional psychological conflict can be created when the child is criticized by teachers and parents as "dumb." He then loses self-esteem, that is, what little self-esteem he may possess.

One nine-year-old boy was brought to me because he was unable to learn and also was very disruptive in school. He had been raised by an aunt and had never known his mother, who had been confined in a mental hospital since his birth.

His aunt told me the boy had serious difficulty falling asleep and that whenever she entered his bedroom, even late at night, he would still be awake. In school he created a continuous disturbance and was constantly involved in fights with other children, losing his temper readily.

The aunt told me that the boy's mother—her sister—behaved very much as the boy did. She, too, had been unable to sleep and was continuously sent home from school as a problem child.

"Have you told the boy this?" I asked.

"Of course," she answered in surprise, as though it was his right to know.

Here we see the boy's identification with his unknown mother, who also had been an underachiever and unruly in school. This was probably all he knew about her, judging from

162

the aunt. Unfortunately, when a young person lives with relatives, he is apt to learn more quickly about the faults of his parents rather than the virtues. The knowledge of faults frequently creates resentment for being saddled with parental characteristics which the youngster considers a handicap, limiting his capabilities. He may take revenge in delinquent behavior, thus punishing both the critical relatives and the absent parents. Also, he may hate his relatives for daring to criticize his parents, whom he must protect, in one sense, to maintain his own identity.

Some youths may be more emotionally disturbed than they appear. In manic-depressive illness there occurs an interim interval, between the manic period when a person is elated and the depressed phase when he cannot function and feels suicidal. During this interim interval, a young person will appear normal and you do not suspect the deeper illness unless you are aware of the extreme limits of the fluctuating moods.

I have discovered that a number of children and youths with manic-depressive qualities come from families where one parent is manic-depressive. Sometimes the young person is berated for the very moods the parent himself exhibits.

Schizophrenia is easier for the lay person to recognize because there is no interim interval when the person appears normal. As I said earlier, there may be many types of schizophrenia. Sometimes a murderer may be schizophrenic, for some schizophrenics act out their anger, although many do not.

I am reminded of a young man of nineteen whom I saw briefly when I worked in the prison ward at Bellevue Hospital. Diagnosed as schizophrenic, he had stabbed to death an eighteen-year-old girl.

When I interviewed him I asked, "Why did you kill her?"

163

"I was in love with her," he said, as though that were a perfectly normal reason for murdering someone.

"Why would you kill her if you loved her?" I asked.

"She cheated on me," he replied. "She took another man to her apartment."

"Do you know who the other man was?"

"No. I never asked her."

"Don't you think you should have asked her? It might have been a relative or friend."

"I couldn't ask her. I never spoke to her in my life."

"Never spoke to her?" I was amazed at this revelation.

"Never said a word to her."

This was similar to the story told in John Fowles's *The Collector*. In this book a young man in England daily follows a young woman, knows her every move, finally speaks to her and persuades her to come home with him. He keeps her prisoner until she finally dies of pneumonia when he refuses to bring a doctor to the house.

Here in the heart of New York the same tragedy had been enacted. This young victim never even knew the identity of the man who killed her because he thought he loved her, and was too frightened to speak to her but, in his deranged mind, acted as though she belonged to him.

"How well did you know her?" I needed some details to make sense of his brutal act.

"For two years I watched her every move. She lived across the court from me in the next apartment building. She kept the shades up most of the time. She had long black hair and she was beautiful and I loved her. I followed her to the subway every morning and waited for her when she came home at night. She was always alone. Until she started bringing this strange young man home. Then I couldn't stand it. I had to kill her."

164

Although I knew nothing of this young man's background, I could sense that here was an anger at parents, particularly his mother (since he killed a woman), that knew no bounds. We might guess he had a very seductive mother and that he was violently jealous of his father, since what sparked the murder was the young woman's attraction to another man.

The young person who does not act out his anger but keeps it within may show signs of it in what we call psychosomatic illness.

A youth of nineteen came to see me because he had broken out with hives all over his body, including his throat. His doctor suspected the cause might be emotional.

I asked, "When did you start getting hives?"

"About two weeks ago," he responded.

"Is this the first time?"

"The first," he said. He could hardly speak, so sore was his throat.

But I had to get answers to some questions if I was to help him. "What happened in your life about two weeks ago?" I asked.

He thought for a moment, then said, "My fiancée and I had a fight. We made up afterwards, but we had quite an argument."

"Can you tell me about it?"

"We were eating in a restaurant and in the booth next to us sat three very handsome young men. I admit I'm very jealous of Linda, but she gives me cause to be. She was flirting with them. I didn't want to make a scene, so I didn't say anything but I could hardly wait for them to leave. After they were gone I asked why she insisted on making me jealous. She was indignant and said she was just being polite, when they smiled at her it was easier to smile back than to act offended or make a fuss. One word led to another. I took her

165

home and left her there without saying good night. In the morning I woke up with the hives."

"As you left her, how did you feel toward her?" I asked.

"I wanted to kill her," he said through clenched teeth.

"And how did you feel towards the three handsome men in the booth?"

"I could cheerfully have killed them, too," he replied.

"Instead you broke out with hives," I pointed out. "You turned your violence on yourself."

He smiled shamefacedly. "I didn't realize at the time how angry I felt. All I knew was I thought Linda was baiting me."

"Don't you trust her?" I asked.

"I don't trust any woman," he said bitterly.

"Why is that?"

"I was engaged once before and I found out the girl was two-timing me behind my back with her boss."

"But that doesn't mean all women would cheat on you."

"I don't trust *any* woman," he repeated.

"Maybe you choose the woman you know will cheat on you," I suggested.

"Why would I do that?" His voice held alarm.

"Perhaps you do not really want to get married yet. So you pick a woman you will be sure somehow will get you out of the engagement. She does something to hurt you and then you can justifiably break it."

"I don't know about that." He sounded angry, and a trifle bewildered.

"The way you tell it your fiancée *was* flirting with those three men."

"I know damn well she was," he muttered.

"So you have reason not to trust her."

He was getting more and more annoyed, with his feelings

166

now directed toward me. But I did not mind. I knew the stronger the emotion of anger became, the sooner the hives would vanish. And by the time he returned for a second session, they were gone. We talked now of his rage at a mother he felt never trusted him and, at the same time, made him feel she did not want to lose him to another woman.

A story is often related in psychiatric circles to show the connection between repressed anger and psychosomatic illness. A man suffered from severe arthritis in his right arm which refused to respond to medication. His physician finally suggested he be hypnotized and, while under hypnosis, receive instructions to believe the arm was cured.

The man went to a hypnotist who did as the physician suggested. He told the man as he sat in a trance, "You no longer suffer from arthritis. When you wake up, your arm will be completely healed and you can use it as you would normally."

As the man came out of his trance, he found, to his surprise, that all pain had disappeared from his right arm and he could use it freely.

He went home, where he lived with a selfish, nagging wife who was always berating him for not earning enough money and for not being "a man." The next morning when he awoke, he went down to the kitchen, seized a long bread knife, walked upstairs to the bedroom. There he plunged the knife into his wife's heart with the right arm, the arm that, the day before, had been so paralyzed he could not lift it.

In other words, the unconscious part of his mind had protected him against committing a violent act by paralyzing his right arm. This is how our psychic defenses work in our behalf, to keep us from hurting ourselves or others. Unable to cope with his great anger at his wife, unable to bring himself to get psychiatric help, he had immobilized that part of his body that would have harmed her and himself, for he knew he would go to prison if he murdered her.

Our body and mind work as a unit, one complementing the other. When we feel a sensation in our body, some part of our mind reacts. If we feel a painful sensation, our mind will use its full strength to protect our body from hurt. In the same way, when we suffer a severe psychic blow, our body will come to the rescue of our mind. Mind and body work together for our physical and psychological survival.

"Conversion" is the term Freud used to describe how an instinctual wish (the wish to kill, the wish to have sexual relations with some forbidden figure such as a parent) can be changed into physical symptoms so that psychic anxiety will be less. It is the function of what is known as "repression," another psychic process, to see that our unconscious wishes, if they are too threatening, do not get through to consciousness (such as the hypnotized man's wish to kill his wife). Or, if they do, that they are disguised in such form as physical illness, which also serves as punishment for the forbidden wish. You cannot say the human mind is not economical!

That emotional forces can affect our body has been demonstrated by the experiments of Dr. Hans Selye of Montreal, among others. Dr. Selye has shown that stress can produce illness. Using animals, he reported extensive damage to their bodies, both neurologically and chemically, when they were exposed to stimuli that made them very frightened. The "stress syndrome," as he called it, led to pathological changes and, in some cases, even to the death of the animal.

Physical illness may be our compromise with a wish. Unconscious desire is not completely denied, yet its aim and object are changed so that it is no longer so dangerous (the man with

168

the hives did not murder others but he inflicted less serious harm on himself).

Indigestion may be a symptom of our disgust and contempt for someone, or perhaps we would like to vomit up some thought or wish that disturbs us. Constipation may be an expression of resentment at the idea of parting from someone or something we cherish (as we, as infants, cherished our feces).

Headaches, colds, fainting fits, and convulsive seizures may symbolize in the unconscious the climax of sexual intercourse or a fantasied sexual attack: pains in legs or arms may relate to a hostility one dares not admit openly to the self. Feelings that have been repressed thus make themselves known in oblique fashion, decipherable not to the patient but to the psychiatrist. The psychiatrist can then help the patient face the emotions he is repressing and the need for the physical illness will disappear.

When one of the organs of the body serves both an erotic and physiological function, such as the mouth, stomach, skin, rectum, or genitals, intense erotic fantasies we have involving it may affect its physiological functioning. A nonsexual part of the body may also be used to represent symbolically a sexual part. Thus the nose, an appendage that juts out, may stand for the penis in the unconscious, or the ear may represent the vagina.

Dr. Georg Groddeck, in his classic book *The Unknown Self,* writing eloquently of the relationship between emotions and psychosomatic illness, said:

Let us take the common expression, "I have caught a cold." In these words, does anybody ever realize the contradiction implied to the commonly accepted theory of the causation of disease? That it is not the chill from outside that brings about the illness, but that it is I, the person who gets ill, who makes use of this or that nameless cause, in order to make myself ill by its means? We have the same implication in such phrases as "He has broken his leg," "He has got pneumonia," "He has caught such and such an infection;" in all of these there is the idea that the man intentionally makes himself ill, that he seizes any opportunity that offers to harm himself. From this standpoint, the expression "I catch a cold" is comparable to "I cut my throat."

Psychosomatic illness relieves a sense of guilt. In Groddeck's words:

> Sickness, and this is an allurement very hard to withstand, makes us innocent; the sick man has no consciousness of guilt, or at least he has a means of destroying it, for he may become worse and worse and at last carry matters so far that he loses consciousness altogether, and with it all feeling of responsibility.

Children realize the advantage of falling ill. Their mother must now take care of them, instead of blaming them for what they may have done wrong.

Children and young people often take what psychoanalysis calls "a flight into illness." Groddeck explains this:

> Whoever finds life too hard, sometimes external life, still oftener his private mental life, can easily drop all his difficulties, at least for a time, if he gets ill. The man who breaks his leg cannot go to business, he cannot even be brought into a court of justice until it is possible to move him there without danger, for examination. The man who cannot see which way to take in his mental struggle gets a high fever which deprives him of all power of making a decision, and this perhaps so clouds his consciousness that all remembrance of the inner conflict disappears most opportunely.

Flight into illness offers another essential advantage, he says. It is the most effective means of repression. The man who falls ill not only postpones the solution of his inner conflicts to a future time, but is also able with the help of the illness to repress the conflict so effectively that either it never emerges again or with every fresh illness it is more easily repressed into the depths of the unconscious.

Groddeck points out there is deep significance in the words of Christ to the sick. Instead of talking about cure, Christ says, "Thy sins are forgiven thee."

This remarkable doctor, who was a friend of Freud's and carried psychoanalytic theories into general medicine, expressed simply but eloquently how psychiatry can help ease psychosomatic illness:

> So long as a man lives in anxiety, so long will he show the symptoms of anxiety; no sooner is he convinced that his anxiety is unnecessary than he feels himself healthy.

Psychoanalysis started with psychosomatic illness. The famous Anna O., known as the first patient, was seen by Dr. Josef Breuer, who told Freud of her remarkable cure as she talked month after month about what was troubling her. Originally she was suffering from physical symptoms, including paralysis of legs and arms, poor vision, a wracking cough, and loss of speech. All these symptoms disappeared as she was able to relive traumatic experiences that had occurred in connection with her father's death.

One of Freud's first patients, Fräulein Lucy R., a governess, sought help because of a severe nasal condition which made her feel so depressed and drained that she could not work.

Freud asked her to tell him everything that came to mind.

171

This she did. He then commented it seemed to him she was hopelessly in love with her widowed employer, whose two children were in her care.

"Yes, I think that's true," she admitted.

Freud said in amazement, "But if you knew you loved your employer, why didn't you tell me?"

"I didn't know—or rather I didn't want to know," she replied. "I wanted to drive it out of my head and not think of it again, and I believe latterly I have succeeded."

Freud realized that Fräulein Lucy had tried very hard to forget the deep emotion she felt for her employer. She wanted to repress awareness of her love because it was unrequited and thus painful to think of.

In his study of other patients, Freud found the same psychic force at work. It was one that held back from consciousness memories that caused pain. In spite of Freud's encouragement, it might take a patient months to speak of some crucial experience in his life that had led to emotional turmoil. Even then he might have difficulty recalling the details and how he felt. It was as though he had to keep fighting against the psychic force that barred such memory and such feelings from consciousness. Freud named this psychic force "repression." This theory of repression he called "the foundation-stone on which the whole structure of psychoanalysis rests."

In working with children and young people, this is what often takes time—the breaking down of resistances that operate against remembering the pain of the past. Even children as young as six and seven have developed strong defenses.

Much repression revolves around a child's anger at his parents. To some extent, he has to repress his anger, for he cannot be allowed to go around exploding in wrath whenever he feels like it. If there is no repression of anger in a child, it may come out in violent physical attacks on a parent, even murder of a parent, or a person who symbolizes the parent.

Some children repress their anger at parents very success-fully, as far as the parents are concerned, but then express their anger elsewhere by becoming delinquent or stealing or taking narcotics. Another device employed is falling phys-ically ill, which tells the parent in a sense, "I am furious at you." The illness is unconscious punishment because of the guilt that follows the angry feelings.

I have found, with the psychosomatic illnesses, that as emotional conflicts are aired, the physical symptoms disappear. After all, the belief in this is what got me into psychiatry in the first place. Had I thought otherwise, I might still be living in Tucson and specializing in allergies.

10.
THE REAL
AND THE
UNREAL

TO SUMMARIZE WHAT I HAVE BEEN DISCUSSING, IT MIGHT BE wise to review the reasons for both real and unreal hate on the part of a child or adolescent.

It is important to distinguish between the two, although it is not a question of either-or. Children usually are angry for both real and unreal reasons; the two cannot be separated. And children are often angry because of *many* real (conscious) and unreal (unconscious) reasons. It is the duty of psychiatrists in many instances to help a child or adolescent become aware of the unconscious reasons for hate so he can then confront them once he is aware of them. Against the unconscious, since he is unaware of it, he is helpless—a victim of its relentless drives.

The unreal reasons for hate possess the ring of what psychoanalysts call "psychic reality." They are even more powerful than the real reasons if they are intensely denied.

The real reasons are those in which the parent either consciously or unconsciously is damaging the esteem of the child. He is unable to respect the child's need for emotional fulfillment largely because the parent himself does not feel emotionally fulfilled.

Among the real reasons why a child or young person may feel angry at parents are the following:

(1) Insistence by parents to "Do as I say, not as I do."

(2) Excessive control of the child as though he were a possession of the parents.

(3) Resentment of the child's existence by the parents, who may even wish he had not been born.

(4) Competing with the child, seeing him as a rival, and jealousy of the affection shown him by the other parent.

(5) Abnormally seductive activities in relation to the child.

(6) Lack of affection.

(7) Lack of attention and neglecting the child's need to be listened to and talked to.

(8) Belittling a child's questions, ideas, and dreams.

(9) Lying to the child.

(10) Misinterpretation of a child's reason for behavior (a child may be thought lazy in school, but has a hearing defect, or is very depressed at the thought of the birth of a younger sister or brother).

(11) Failure to let the child grow up.

(12) The use of money and gifts in a power struggle with each other for the love of the child—especially by divorced parents.

(13) Failure of parents to adapt to contemporary customs, such as long hair on boys and blue jeans for girls.

(14) Inconsistency in discipline—punitive one moment, overaffectionate the next.

(15) Striking or beating a child.

(16) Verbal assaults on a child by means of teasing and sarcasm.

(17) Heedlessness to the child's cries for help (the child

175

with obvious anxiety may turn to drug addiction, stealing, sexual excitement).

(18) The presence of extreme emotional problems within parents themselves, such as alcoholism, or promiscuity, and the failure to help themselves, thus inflicting their emotional illness on the child.

(19) Repeated and needless frustrations of a child, over and above the frustrations inherent in early childhood training.

(20) Overindulgence of the child too early in life, beyond what he needs to feel emotionally secure.

Then there are the unreal reasons for a child's hate, which all children possess to some degree:

(1) Unresolved childhood jealousy of the parent of the same sex.

(2) Unresolved childhood jealousy of a brother or a sister.

(3) Inability to relinquish the infant fantasies of omnipotence and belief in magic.

(4) Demand for perfection in the parent, inability to see the parent as a human being with his own emotional needs.

(5) Misinterpretation of "rejection" by a parent.

(6) Excessive need for love, praise, and attention.

(7) Fantasies developed over the years that have little or nothing to do with reality, as to the nature of sexuality.

(8) Unawareness of aggressive and sexual impulses as natural and desirable to a certain degree.

Suggestions as to what parents may do to help their child or adolescent overcome feelings causing them unhappiness have been given throughout the book. In summary, I will emphasize a few points:

Do not overprotect the child but try to allow him a fair share of independence. Remember, he is developing psychically and must be helped to grow in comfort and security. This does not mean a completely permissive attitude toward a child, but rather one of quiet guidance and wise control.

Do not criticize a child constantly. If you disapprove of what he does, try to tell him so gently and constructively, not in a way that will demolish his spirit and make him hate you.

Do not "undersupport" him but try to be there whenever he needs you, whether it is a major or minor crisis in his life.

Do not shout or scream at a child. Try to control your temper when you feel angry, at the same time not denying to yourself that you *are* angry. You do not have to act on all your emotions, but it is important to be aware of them.

Do not *blame* yourself or the child. It is never a matter of blame but of understanding. Nobody changes for the better through blame.

Be consistent in your discipline. If your own methods of discipline fail to get response from the child, seek advice, either for him or yourself. A little professional guidance may go a long way. You do not have to undertake an extensive psychoanalysis or an indeterminate amount of psychotherapy. Often a few sessions will constitute a turning point. I have seen this happen frequently in my work.

Most important, the parent should try to set an example through what he does rather than preaching. To quote an old proverb:

"Children are more in need of example than in need of advice."

I have much hope where children and parents are concerned. The very fact that a parent will bring his child or adolescent to psychiatrists for help is a sign of hope. The minute a child or young person walks through the door I take this as a signal he wants to get better even though he may be there on order of his parent or the family doctor.

It is heartening to realize some youths are determined to obtain assistance. Sometimes they are even overdetermined.

A nineteen-year-old youth who had called for an appointment walked into my office one afternoon and announced, "I've come all the way from Chicago to see you."

"How did you get my name?" I asked.

"One of my classmates at the university told me about the shrink he had in New York when he was in high school. That was you. I'd like to come to you for help."

"But there are very good psychiatrists in Chicago. Why don't you let me recommend someone there?"

"I don't mind flying here. I've nothing else to do."

"But you're in college there. And it costs a lot of money to fly from Chicago to New York and back."

"All I have is money."

"What do you mean?" I was puzzled.

"I have no family. I'm an orphan. My mother and father died in an automobile crash when I was seven years old and I inherited their fortune. If you don't want to take me because I live in Chicago, I'll simply move to New York and go to a university here."

I was flattered by such allegiance, but not surprised, for one of the highest recommendations—and it is a frequent one—is for some young person who has been helped to tell another about the "shrink" who made his life easier.

In this case I managed to persuade the young would-be traveler to accept the names of several Chicago psychiatrists. I urged him to interview them and decide to which one he wished to go. I assume, since I heard nothing further from him, that he found someone with whom he could work.

In contrast to this experience, it is often incumbent upon me to work to obtain someone's trust so that he can use what a psychiatrist offers. Sometimes a young person will feel he is not worthy of help. Sometimes he is so frightened he will not admit he can use help and covers his fear with false bravado. Sometimes he will not accept assistance because his parents wish him to do so and his deep anger at them prevents him from helping himself.

One factor that impresses me as I work with troubled children and youth is the utter loneliness of most of them. Beneath the anger, beneath the bravado, beneath the role-playing, lies fierce loneliness. They feel they haven't a friend in the world; they feel nobody really cares what happens to them, much less their parents.

Some children seem to need excessive praise and love, beyond that which a parent should be expected to offer. For one reason or another, these children feel exceptionally nervous and insecure, are afraid to trust their own judgment, and show a lack of confidence in themselves.

A fourteen-year-old boy, his face broken out in acne and forty pounds overweight, told me, "My mother and father never praise anything I do. I might as well be an orphan."

"Don't they ever show signs of loving you?" I asked.

He pursed his lips, admitted, "Well, sometimes."

"What times are those?" I asked.

"If I get good marks in school. Or when I go on a diet and lose weight."

"Parents can't spend all their time praising you," I pointed out. "And sometimes the greatest praise is in a look or a smile or a kiss."

"I never thought of that," he said in wonder. "My mother does smile at me a lot."

I think we have to face the sad truth that nobody seems

179

to get all the love he feels he deserves! The need of a child for love and admiration is insatiable; he will take every bit of love and attention he can get, and then ask for more.

Sometimes a child feels unloved when the facts, if he only knew them, prove otherwise. A ten-year-old girl was sent to me by her family physician because she had severe stomach aches with no physical cause.

"Are you unhappy about any particular thing at this time?" I asked her.

She hesitated, then said, "My mother doesn't like me any more."

"What makes you say that?" I asked.

"She's sending me away," said the little girl sadly.

"What do you mean?" I asked.

"She doesn't want me around any longer. I'm being sent to boarding school," she replied.

I called up the mother, told her what her daughter had said. The mother explained, also in a sad voice, "I don't want to tell her this, but I have to go to a sanitarium for several months because of tuberculosis, and I think she'd be better off in a private school, and so does my husband."

"Tell her the truth," I said. "She feels you don't want her any more. If she knows the truth, she'll feel relieved. Those stomach aches will probably disappear."

"Can she take the truth?" asked the mother worriedly.

"It's far easier for her to take the reality of your tuberculosis than the fantasy that you do not love her any longer," I said.

Children usually can cope with reality, harsh though it may be, far easier than they can cope with the frightening fantasies that whirl through their minds when they feel rejected, even though they actually are not. If they actually *are* rejected, that is, abandoned by parents or treated brutally, this is another matter.

I believe parents should provide psychiatric help for a child the moment they see him becoming very irritable, angry, lazy, inattentive, withdrawn, or rebellious in any way. Parents should seek help not only for the child's future happiness but for the sake of their own peace of mind. No parent feels comfortable around an angry child.

Angry children do not have to stay angry if they are guided toward an understanding of the reasons for their anger —both the real and the unreal.

"What are you going to do to make me better?" demanded a fourteen-year-old boy during a consultation. "I don't want you to change me. I want to be me."

"You will never be anybody else but you," I replied. "But here your real self will be brought out. It has been hidden behind your anxieties and depressions."

He looked puzzled. I explained further. "The most fascinating research you can do is to discover yourself, to analyze your own personality, to know what made you what you are and find out what you want to be—strong, secure, happy, wealthy, whatever. This can only be done if we work together in an effort to bring out the real you, the one in which you can take pride."

Children and young people are always very grateful for the help they receive. They express their gratitude in different ways, sometimes with words, sometimes with small gifts. Psychoanalysts are not supposed to accept gifts from patients—it is gift enough that the patient gets better—but I make exceptions in the case of children whose feelings would be hurt if I refused to take their offerings.

For Christmas last year, a fourteen-year-old girl handed

me a scrapbook of red and green paper on whose pages she had pasted cartoons collected from various magazines dealing with therapy. One from the *New Yorker* showed a man and woman at a cocktail party, the woman saying to the man, "You mean you *think* you had a happy childhood."

Another, also from the *New Yorker* (that magazine's cartoonists certainly are given a chance to express their hostility toward analysts), pictured two psychoanalysts, each lying on a couch, holding up their notebooks, as one says to the other, "I'll tell you my-y-y dreams, you tell me your-r-rs. . . ."

Some parents thank me after a youngster has been helped. They say, "It's such a pleasure to live with my child now."

But some resent a youngster getting better. This may mean they cannot dictate to him or bully him as they once did.

One father complained about his son, after the youth had been in treatment a year, "He's a worse bum than before. He won't talk to his mother or me now. He's got you."

For his first session the fifteen-year-old boy had dragged himself into my office like a sheep dog. He had dropped out of school and gone on pot. Within the year of help, he was back in school, alert and getting high marks, off the pot and determined to go to college. But all his father was concerned about was that the boy was becoming more independent, which the father resented.

Parents also may become jealous of a child's attachment to the therapist, not realizing it is necessary for the child to cooperate so he can abandon harmful behavior. It takes time for the parents to understand that the child will love them all the more as he breaks free of their control.

This book may seem to lower the psychic boom on parents. I could just as well have looked at the emotional lives of parents and, learning of their sorrows and fears and angers,

182

come up with a sympathetic portrayal of parents saying of *their* parents, "I hate my parents!"

But you have to start someplace in the psychic chain that leads from generation to generation back to Adam and Eve (was not Cain the first angry child?) in trying to understand what produces anger in a child. And since I have treated so many children and adolescents, it is with them I have started, always remembering, however, that the parent does the very best he can, that almost all parents love their children and wish them well in a conscious sense, and the unconscious problems they visit on their children they cannot help.

We have to help our troubled youth. They are the next generation. We have to release them from their anger. Otherwise, the nation and the world will suffer. As we help children and adolescents to happier futures, we help the world to a happier future.